H o w

Haw

DATE DUE

SEP 1 0 1996	
AUG 2 7 1996	
SEP 1 9 1996	
SEP 2 6 1996	
NOV 0 5 1996	
JAN 2 1 1997	
FEB 0 7 1997	
FEB 2 7 1997	
MAR 1 3 1997	
MAR 2 4 2001	
APR 2 1 2001	

DEMCO, INC. 38-2931

THE HOW-TO-SPOT SERIES

How To Spot Hawks & Eagles, by Clay Sutton and Patricia Taylor Sutton
How To Spot An Owl, by Patricia and Clay Sutton
How To Spot A Fox, by J. David Henry

Hawks & Eagles

Clay Sutton and
Patricia Taylor Sutton

CHAPTERS PUBLISHING LTD., SHELBURNE, VERMONT 05482

598.916

Published by
Chapters Publishing Ltd.
2031 Shelburne Road
Shelburne, Vermont 05482

Library of Congress Cataloguing-in-Publication Data

Sutton, Clay.
    How to spot hawks & eagles / Clay Sutton and Patricia Taylor Sutton.
       p.   cm. — (The How to spot series)
    Includes bibliographical references and index.
    ISBN 1-57630-001-3 (hardcover). — ISBN 1-57630-000-5 (softcover)
    1. Hawks—North America. 2. Eagles—North America. 3. Bird
watching—North America.
    I. Sutton, Patricia. II. Title. III. Series.
    QL696.F32S97 1996
    598.9'16—dc20   95-53782

Printed and bound in Canada by Metropole Litho
St. Bruno de Montarville, Quebec

Designed by Eugenie Seidenberg Delaney

Front cover: Golden Eagle photograph by Keith A. Szafranski

8|96

Pwr

For Roger Tory Peterson
and for all those who came before.
May the contributions of the elders
always be recognized and ever appreciated.

Contents

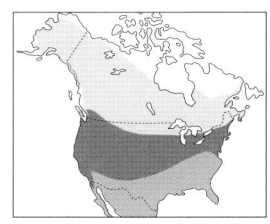

Key to Range Maps

Breeding Range

Permanent Range

Winter Range

Note: *Since female raptors are generally larger than their respective males, sizes (length and wingspan) are averages. The size of various subspecies may vary as well.*

Acknowledgments

T O LIST ALL of the individuals and groups throughout North America who have contributed to our understanding of birds of prey and raptor migration would require a book at least equal in length to this one. When Maurice Broun first scaled the ridge at Hawk Mountain over 50 years ago, virtually nothing was known of either hawk migration or even hawk identification. When Floyd Wolfarth crested Raccoon Ridge there were, for example, few golden eagle records in the East. When Roger Tory Peterson, James Allen and James Tanner established the watch at Cape May in 1937 as an adjunct to their warden duties, hawks were still being identified along the barrels of shotguns.

Few today can appreciate how little was known before the pioneers of hawkwatching raised binoculars instead of guns. Birders today, in knowing when, where and how to spot hawks and eagles, owe them a great deal, for 50 years ago raptor watching was indeed in its infancy.

On these solid foundations, watchers today add building blocks. Each watch site, manned every season by dedicated volunteers, adds to our knowledge of hawks and hawkwatching. We owe a debt of gratitude to those hundreds, indeed thousands, of enthusiasts—this book could not have been written without them.

For sharing in our passion for hawks and eagles and joining us on raptor travels, thanks to: Sheri Williamson and Tom Wood, Dave Sibley and Joan Walsh, Ray Schwartz, Else and Wayne Greenstone, Harry Darrow, Arnie Moorhouse, Tony Leukering, Louise Zemaitis, Alec Humann, Frank Nicoletti, Dave Wiedner, Jon Sutton, Jim Watson, Jack and Jesse Connor, Wendy and Dennis Allen, Jim and Deb Dowdell, Vince Elia, Bill Glaser, Dave Ward, Jane and Bill Ruffin, Andrés Sada, Paul Kosten and Karen Williams, Sharon Taylor, B.J. Gerhart, Mitch Smith, Jane Galetto, Tony and Leslie Ficcaglia, Dan O'Connor, Al Nicholson and Pete Dunne.

We have spent many pleasant hours watching hawks, and having "hawk talks" with Harry LeGrand, Fred Hamer, Jeff Bouton, Jorge Montejo Diaz, Bill Clark, Brian Wheeler, Fred Mears, Chris Schultz, Jerry Liguori, Frank

Nicoletti, Tom Laura, Bob Barber, Rosemarie Widmer, Sandy Sherman, Gerry Smith, Ned and Linda Harris, Walter Fritton, Brian Sullivan, Bill Seng, Paul Kerlinger, Paul Lehman and Shawneen Finnegan, Joe and Sandy Usewicz, Dick Walton, Brett Ewald, Laurie Goodrich, Tom Laura, John Economidy, Fred Tilly, Bobby Squires, Richard Crossley, Kathleen and Thane Maynard, Hal Cohen, Jim Brett and the late Harold Axtell. We thank you all. We have learned much and have loved every minute.

We thank all those who have put so much time and effort into HMANA, the Hawk Migration Association of North America, and wish particularly to thank Jeff Dodge and Miriam Moore for their yeoman efforts. Thanks also to our fellow members of the Delaware Valley Ornithological Club. Alan Fish, Keith Bildstein, Steve Hoffman, Jeff Dodge, Sheri Williamson and Tom Wood provided key information about their organizations and learning opportunities. Dave Wiedner helped immensely in compiling the draft migration data. We thank Paul Lehman for reviewing and strengthening our manuscript.

Tom Gilmore, Director of the New Jersey Audubon Society, Pete Dunne, Director of the Cape May Bird Observatory, and Bob Zappalorti, Executive Director of Herpetological Associates, supported this project at every step. John Winklemann was the professor who put Clay on that dune in Mexico so many years ago. Thanks for the opportunity and guidance, John.

Pat thanks her parents, George and Mary Taylor, and Clay remembers his parents for putting us on the road to discovery. Finally, we owe so much to Bill Bailey, Ed Manners and Al Nicholson, our natural history and raptor mentors, for walking with us so much farther down that road. Who knows where we would be without all of you.

Foreword

BY JACK CONNOR, AUTHOR OF *SEASON AT THE POINT*

ICE AND A HARD WIND on the river this morning—and not much to see along the marsh road where I walk my dog: a line of deer tracks in frozen mud, a couple of blackbirds, winter grasses bending and blowing under a cloudless sky. It's too cold today, I am thinking; time to call back the dog and head home. Then, 50 yards in front of me, a hawk swoops across the road. It's a harrier, tilting left and right in the wind, rufous belly catching the light, white rump patch flashing, long legs tucked below. Let the dog run, I decide; it's a good day to be outdoors.

Nothing beats a hawk to stir the blood. Just saying their names out loud can warm you up: harrier, osprey, kestrel, goshawk, caracara. Finding one out in the field is even better, of course. A red-tail perches in a pine tree, a rough-leg rides a thermal, a peregrine stoops on a flock of shorebirds—and who can look away? A single sighting can stay in the mind for a lifetime, as all of us who have been fortunate enough to see a golden eagle or swallow-tailed kite know very well.

Hawks fly high, however, and are wary.

Their plumages make identification a challenge, and their ecology, behavior and geographic distribution are complex. They are not a group mastered in a few months, or even a year or two.

And so we have the book you hold in your hands, by Clay and Pat Sutton, writers, photographers, teachers, raptor experts and the most engaging pair of naturalists I have ever met. For more than 20 years, Clay and Pat have been at the center of the hawkwatching culture in North America, studying birds on the Cape May peninsula and elsewhere across the country, leading dozens of workshops and hundreds of field trips, working ceaselessly for habitat conservation and, in the process, touching the lives of thousands of birders lucky enough to meet them.

Now they have given us *How to Spot Hawks & Eagles*, the perfect companion to their *How To Spot An Owl*. Like that book, this is a compendium of wisdom and current knowledge about the group of birds so many of us love and all naturalists want to know better.

Enjoy. And may your next hawk be a close one.

Preface

Raptors, or birds of prey, are the only group of birds, besides gamebirds, that has attracted a following beyond birdwatchers. A duck hunter in a sodden duck blind will watch with fascination a harrier or marsh hawk patrolling the marsh. A surf fisherman, plying a lonely barrier strand, will pause to watch a hunting fish hawk or osprey plunge into the ocean. City office workers will gather at windows to peer at nesting peregrines on a building ledge. Indeed, hawks and eagles have attracted a near fanatical following all over North America, and thousands of watchers gather at various lookouts each autumn and spring to chart the progress of hawk migration.

Many of these people rarely watch other birds, or do so only casually. Hawks and eagles capture the imagination and wonder of the watcher like no other group of birds. It is not necessarily a beauty of plumage that does this—most North American hawks are subtly patterned with the brown and tan hues of a snow-free winter landscape. Yet in flight, raptors portray a drama, an ease of movement that captivates. While eagles are clearly powerful, bold, and often called majestic, a male sharp-shinned hawk is hardly larger than a robin. Yet even a sharp-shinned hawk shows an efficacy, an energy, a competency that is undeniable to watchers. If not lord of all they survey, raptors as top predators clearly influence and energize their environment in a dynamic way.

Even though I grew up in Cape May and was vaguely aware of the birdwatchers along the roadsides each fall, I saw my first raptor (at least the first one I remember well) in the vast dunes along the Pacific Ocean near the Mexican town of Tonalà in Chiapas. While afield with my father, I had seen the circling red-tailed hawks he pointed out, but never with binoculars or with much interest. I was focusing my attention on fish and pheasants.

It took college, ecology courses and an unpaid job as a research assistant (studying bats in southern Mexico) for me to appreciate my first raptor. We worked mostly in caves, rain forest and farmland, but one weekend we went to the coast for some relaxation. One afternoon, as the others were swimming, I watched (with binoculars in hand) a white-tailed kite hunt the dunes against the setting sun over the Pacific. I stared, mesmerised, as the kite coursed the dunes, hovering and gliding. That evening, it was easy for me to find its distinctive plumage in the Mexican bird guide. From that day on, I became a birder—but one with a primary interest in raptors.

Returning home, I began to discover the world of raptors around me. A visit to Forsythe (Brigantine) National Wildlife Refuge yielded what, to this day, is still my best American kestrel photograph. Within a few weeks, at an Izaak Walton League meeting, I had a chance encounter with the local raptor guru, Al Nicholson. To my surprise, he wanted to see the kestrel photo. He seemed pleased, then, to my delight, inquired if I would like to "go up to Cumberland County to see the nesting bald eagles." The following weekend found me following Al through Bear Swamp, slogging through knee-deep water looking for the right vista, the right angle through the trees where you could see the ancient pine with the venerable eagle's nest silhouetted against the sky about a mile away. At that time, because of DDT, it was the only eagle's nest left in New Jersey.

We saw the eagles, four in fact, two adults and two immatures. With Al, you had to earn your visions. During the day-long trek through the swamp, I saw the same "landmark" tree four times. We were not lost; it was just that Al wanted me to earn the sighting of my first eagles and to appreciate the enormity and wildness of the eagle's home. I've never forgotten that lesson or that long, rainy—yet uplifting—March day.

Once you have spotted your first hawks and eagles, you begin to learn the clues about when, where and how to look. Seven months after the eagle-nest outing, I was prompted to search for golden eagles. Al had instructed, "After leaden gales, look for goldens in the garden," meaning that to see a golden eagle at Cape May, you should scan Pond Creek Marsh on northwest winds the second day after a cold front has passed through. I had recently seen my first broad-winged hawk "kettle" (flock) of about 400 birds, and enthused by that sighting, I anxiously waited at Pond Creek Marsh. After about 20 minutes, among the red-tailed hawks, a larger dark shape appeared. The bird came on, then began soaring. For the first time ever, I saw the distinctive wing pattern of a young golden eagle. This was another pivotal event in my raptor career. On that day, I began a lifelong quest.

In this book, we hope to share with you the lessons that began on a cold March day in 1974. The excitement in searching for hawks, whether nesting birds, winter raptor concentrations or migrants, is that there is always a mystery, an unsolved problem. Could the Cooper's hawk seen today nest near here? Is it going to be a good rough-legged hawk winter? Will this cold front bring the big broad-winged hawk push? I hope you enjoy the search as much as we do, and I invite you to continue the quest with us.

—*Clay Sutton*
Cape May, New Jersey

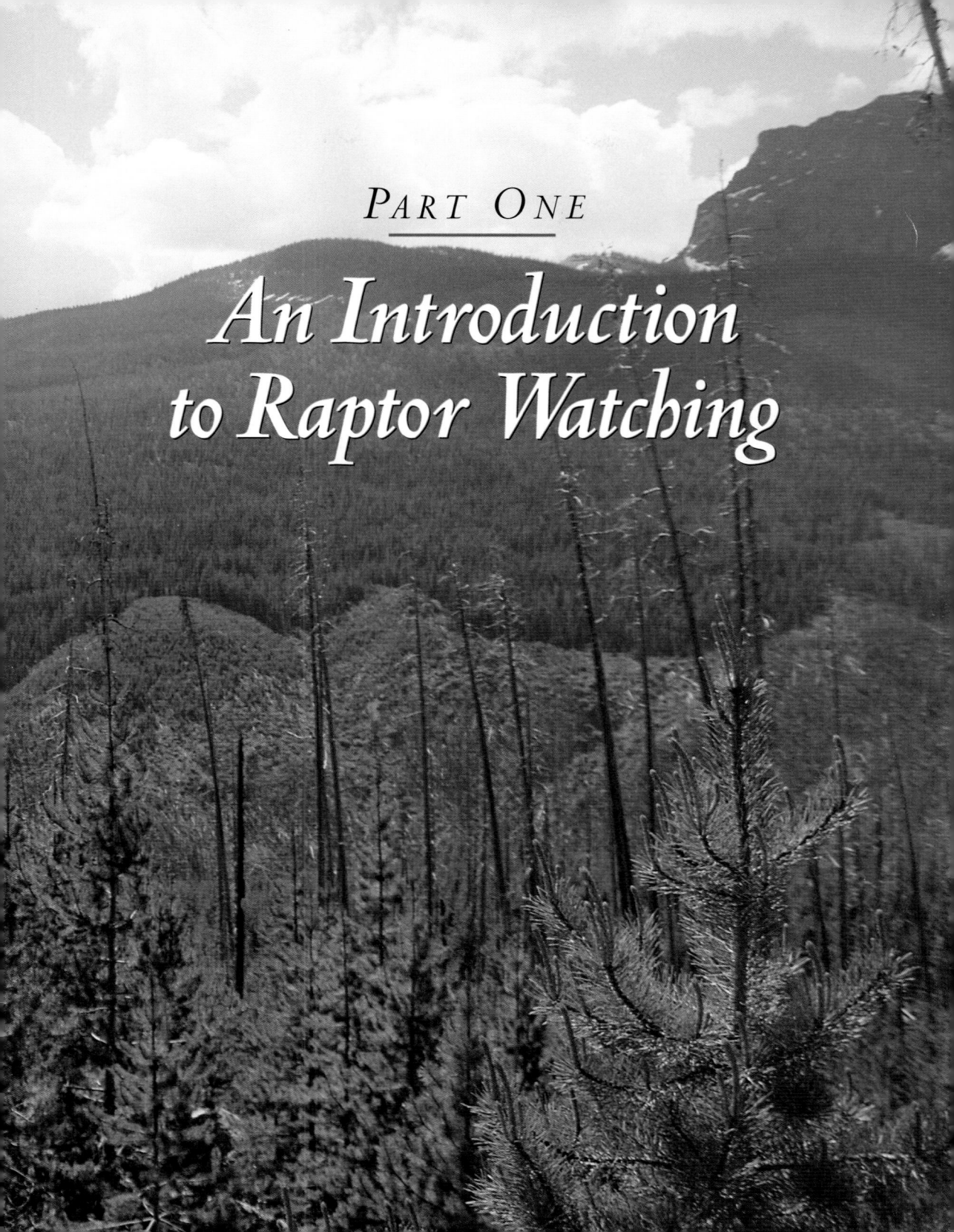

PART ONE

An Introduction to Raptor Watching

Raptor Basics

ETTING THERE had not been easy. It had taken some creative calendar planning and a long drive up from a speaking engagement in Cincinnati. As we neared Madison, Wisconsin, the sleet on the windshield told us that a cold front was moving through. Experience and the weather reports predicted that the next several days would be clear and cold. We met Clay's cousin, Jon, in Madison that night, and as we packed the car at 3:00 A.M. for the final leg of the journey, snow covered the ground but the stars shone brightly in a crystalline sky.

Our destination was Duluth, Minnesota, a legendary location for spotting hawks during their autumn migration. Here, hawks racing south ahead of the coming Canadian winter run into Lake Superior. Because hawks are not accustomed, or designed, to fly over water, they follow the shoreline of the lake, and at the west end, they turn south to enter the United States. Their concentrations above Hawk Ridge overlooking Duluth can be spectacular. It was the first week of November, and we hoped that seasonality and geography would combine to create a magnificent raptor spotting opportunity.

Following directions, we found the Hawk Ridge overlook by about 9:00 A.M. The morning was cold, bitter cold, with racing gray and white puffy clouds overhead. Dressed in all the clothes we had packed, we found some comfort in having the sun in our faces and the wind at our backs. Because of the cold, it took some time for the

Some rewards of spotting: a northern goshawk, *above,* a red-tailed hawk, *right*. Previous pages: scanning for raptors in the Canadian Rockies.

How to Spot Hawks & Eagles

day's flight to develop, often the case in late-season hawkwatching. (In general, raptors rarely require the early rise needed to see migrating songbirds. Think of migrating raptors as solar-powered.)

The view from the hawkwatch at Duluth, Minnesota.

Steady flocks of purple finches, evening and pine grosbeaks, redpolls and Bohemian waxwings flashed by the lookout. Solitary and then small flocks of ravens began coming on. At Duluth, the birds leave a ridge to the east, cross a small valley, then pick up the ridge again right at the hawkwatch. In northwest winds, this topography assures good views of the birds of prey as they catch the updraft off the cliff face.

The hawk flight began slowly, but rapidly picked up, with a few birds always in sight. Being late in the season, we were not seeing the thousands of broad-winged and sharp-shinned hawks for which Duluth is famous in September, but we were looking for late-season hawks: red-tails, rough-legs and goshawks. The birds appeared as specks over the far ridge and then came on, alternately gliding and flapping toward us until they appeared directly overhead. On they came, light red-tails, dark red-tails and all ages and forms of rough-legs. Eagles came with them, sometimes out over the town and harbor, sometimes high above us. Then, out of nowhere, a young golden eagle was circling with three rough-legs right over our heads. The goshawks came low, usually skimming the trees out in front, then cresting the ridge, often at point-blank range. The brown youngsters blended with the somber trees, but the colors of the silvery adults seemed to anticipate the coming winter. Some sightings were brief, others prolonged as the birds circled overhead, but being migrants, they all too soon disappeared over the town. Here, at the end of the intervening lake, they could finally make the turn and continue their long journey south.

By the time we left the ridge that late afternoon, cold but satisfied, we had seen more bald eagles, rough-legs and goshawks than one could see in several seasons back home in Cape May, New Jersey, often called the raptor capital of North America. In Cape May, the hawkwatch averages 60,000 birds of prey each fall. But Duluth, far to the north and west, had yielded a far different mix of raptors than we see in the East.

Spotting different species of hawks and finding them in large numbers often means one must travel. To plan this trip, we had pored over many years of hawk migration counts from Duluth (where an official counter logs the flights each day for Friends of Hawk Ridge Reserve). We learned that peak flights for adult goshawks and rough-legs, our target species, usually occur during the first week of November. The fortuitous timing of a strong cold front, clear skies and brisk winds created a memorable day of hawkwatching. We have yearned to return ever since.

While Duluth is certainly one of the premier places in the U.S. to spot hawks and eagles, there are few places in North America where one is far from either migrating, resident or wintering hawks (those that spend the winter in one area, then migrate north in the spring to their nesting grounds). Opportunities to watch raptors occur even in urban areas. San Francisco hosts a well-known hawkwatching destination, and New York City has several good spots as well. By applying the parameters of planning, seasonality and weather conditions, one can find hawks and eagles almost anywhere in North America, and probably close to where you live.

What Is a Raptor?

WHILE MANY BIRDS kill to eat—robins eat worms, warblers catch insects, terns dive for fish—they are not thought of as birds of prey. More narrowly, birds of prey are those that hunt and eat warm-blooded animals such as rats, mice and smaller birds, and other vertebrates such as snakes, lizards, frogs and fish. Collectively, hawks, eagles, falcons, vultures and owls are birds of prey known as raptors. While owls are nocturnal raptors, all hawks

and eagles are diurnal raptors, active during the day, although some are decidedly crepuscular, active in the dim light of dawn and dusk.

Hawks and eagles are members of the order Falconiformes, comprising approximately 290 species worldwide. Most are hunters, although many are also scavengers. There is little that raptors will not eat: osprey feed on fish, and kestrel often eat small grasshoppers and dragonflies. Friends have told us of watching bald eagles feasting on a whale carcass in Alaska and vultures picking from a dead elephant in Africa. Golden eagles have been witnessed killing prey as large as a pronghorn antelope or wolf, although this is far from the norm.

The size differences in raptors are striking. In North America, there are 34 regularly occurring (nesting) species of raptors, ranging from the female bald eagle, which can attain a wingspan of 7½ feet and a weight of 13.6 pounds, to the male sharp-shinned hawk, with as little as a 20-inch wingspan and a weight of only 3 ounces. This makes the bald eagle more than 70 times heavier than the sharp-shinned hawk. For most raptor species, the females are noticeably larger than the males. There is actually little that sets an eagle apart from a hawk except size, and even then it is a matter of semantics. Europe and Asia, for example, have a number of "eagles" that are no larger than red-tailed hawks.

It is the natural history and behavior of raptors that have fascinated humans for centuries. Their lifespan can be quite long. Bald eagles commonly live over 20 years in the wild, while smaller hawks, like kestrels, normally reach less than half this age. As with most birds, mortality is highest among juveniles; if a hawk makes it past adolescence, it will probably be long-lived.

Raptors, as hunters, generally have expansive home ranges. A bird of prey's territory must be large enough to contain a prey base that will support the adults and the young they raise each year. Most individual raptors occupy the same territory, if not the same nest, year after year. Many mate for life.

Hawks and eagles are known for their spectacular display flights during the breeding season. When attempting to attract a mate or initiate nesting, the males of many species perform elaborate courtship flights. Male northern harriers perform acrobatic loops known as "sky dancing." Eagles will lock talons and perform rolls in unison during courtship. It is not a reach to term such flights exuberant. Raptors care for their young long after fledging, and many teach their young to hunt.

While many raptors are sedentary and never leave their established territory, others are highly migratory. Peregrine falcons breed above the Arctic Circle in Greenland and may winter as far south as Tierra del Fuego, at the southern tip of South America. Swainson's hawks nest northward into central Alaska and winter on the Argentine pampas. It is often their migratory tendencies that make many hawks either hard to spot (for example, the black hawk is only in its limited southwestern U.S. range for about five months before it returns to its Mexican wintering grounds) or easy to spot (huge spatial and temporal concentrations of hawks of many species can be viewed at migratory junctures like Duluth, Minnesota; Hawk Mountain, Pennsylvania;

and Cape May, New Jersey). For many birders, it is the daytime migration spectacle that makes hawks so special.

Adaptations

THE LONG-DISTANCE MIGRATIONS of hawks are made possible by their amazing flight capabilities. Eagles and most hawks are designed for soaring flight. Their wide, blunt wings are called high-lift wings, and the primary feathers have slotting—spaces between successive primaries—which helps maintain lift at low speeds. A soaring bird can maintain or even increase altitude without flapping its wings by using the natural updrafts that occur over cliffs and mountain ridges, or by using thermals. Thermals are rising columns of warm air that form when surfaces such as plowed fields, rocky hillsides and even parking lots are heated by the sun. Because soaring birds must stay within the thermals to gain altitude, they soar upward in spirals. During migration, flocks of hawks, called kettles, are often seen in the same thermal. A "kettle of hawks" refers to hawks boiling up inside a thermal much as steam bubbles up from a kettle of boiling water. Hawks first *soar* in updrafts or thermals, then *glide* from one thermal to the next as soon as the one they are in dissipates. They slowly lose altitude in a glide, but regain it in the next thermal. Raptors use little more energy soaring and gliding than they do when perched. Hawks use flapping flight when necessary—when no lift is available—but flapping flight is not very energy-efficient.

Hawks and eagles are renowned for the al-

With its excellent vision and impressive speed, a red-tailed hawk zeros in on its target.

titude of their flight. Hawks commonly soar 500 to 1,000 feet, and vultures searching for food are reported to reach 10,000 feet regularly. It is calculated that a bird at 500 feet can view 27 square miles of the Earth's surface; at 1,000 feet, 39 square miles. At 5,000 feet, 86 square miles are visible, and at 10,000 feet, an incredible 122 square miles can be seen. At Cape May, soaring broad-winged hawks are sometimes seen disappearing into cloud cover, and migrating osprey are regularly picked up as tiny specks against the clouds with 10x (10-power) binoculars. When soaring, and particularly when migrating, raptors will regularly go beyond the limit of vision, even binocular-aided vision. "Noonday lulls," when migration seems to slow, are well known at hawk-watches, but radar studies show the hawks are still there—high in thermals that are at their strongest during the hours when the sun is hottest. In sunny, hot South Texas, some migrating broad-winged hawks regularly reach 4,600 feet, but radar shows most to be flying around 2,300 feet. In these studies, broad-winged hawks were judged to disappear to the naked eye at about 2,100 feet in a cloudless sky, while a sharp-shinned hawk, a smaller bird, seemed to disappear at about 1,650 feet.

Speeds attained by hawks and eagles are equally impressive. We have seen an adult bald eagle "fly down" a flock of black ducks in level flight and grab one from the flock; the fleeing ducks had probably attained a flight speed of near 60 miles per hour. Falcons, with their long, thin wings, are designed more for speed than for soaring (although they soar perfectly well) and are the fastest of the hawks in level flight. Peregrines pursue their prey in spectac-

Visual and aural acuity: Raptors' keen eyes easily discern hidden prey, _top_. The northern harrier's facial disk reflects sound back to its ears, _bottom_.

ular dives or "stoops" and have been regularly clocked near 90 miles an hour in a dive. While the often-quoted 200 miles an hour dive speeds for peregrines are probably erroneous, speeds of between 120 and 170 miles per hour are thought to be possible. Golden eagles also regularly pursue prey in dives, whether hunting ptarmigan on an Alberta mountainside or waterfowl on a Chesapeake marsh. Because goldens are heavier, they probably attain even greater flight speeds than peregrines—a stooping golden eagle is one of the most awe-inspiring sights in hawkwatching.

Raptors are known for their extraordinary vision. If our eyes were as large, proportionately, as those of an eagle, they would weigh several pounds apiece. It is said that a raptor's vision is about eight times better than that of a human. Their vision is slightly telescopic, but most of the visual acuity is derived from the density of sensory cells on the retinal surface. A soaring eagle can spot a rabbit two miles away. Individual broad-winged hawks can spot each other when seven miles apart; this is how the large, migratory flocks of broad-wings form, by finding each other in coveted thermals.

Raptors also have characteristic beaks and feet. The hawk's hooked upper bill and spoon-like lower one enable it to pierce and tear apart prey. A falcon's beak is notched, for quickly and cleanly severing the neck vertebrae of its primary victims, birds. Raptors have specialized feet, or talons, for catching, holding and carrying prey. A typical raptor foot has four talons; the hind talon is a spearlike killing toe. Eagle talons in particular are extremely stout and powerful. The osprey has specialized barbs on its feet to help hold slippery fish.

How to Spot Hawks & Eagles

Among raptors, only some vultures hunt by sense of smell. Hearing is well developed in hawks and eagles, and is used to locate prey, mates and enemies. The northern harrier uses hearing to a great degree while hunting, and its face is shaped like an owl's to maximize hearing ability (the facial disk reflects sound back to its ears).

Raptor voices are quite variable; while some hawks, such as red-tails and red-shoulders, have loud, harsh or strident calls, the voices of eagles are surprisingly weak.

Types of Raptors

THE TURKEY VULTURES found the Cape May thermal first and began circling in their somewhat haphazard way. One black vulture circled high above them. Nearby, red-tailed and red-shouldered hawks became aware of the thermal and quickly flapped in to join the vultures. This swirling mass soon attracted others—two ospreys, one behind the other, began circling through the vultures. Accipiters converged, several sharp-shins and two Cooper's hawks. A northern harrier paused briefly to gain valuable altitude for its flight across Delaware Bay. As the thermal began to dissipate, a single young broad-winged hawk appeared from nowhere, and a lone merlin circled once, creating a ten-species kettle, our personal best. Mixed-species kettles are actually the rule, not the exception, at Cape May, but this one was special—a kaleidoscope of shapes—ten species of six "types" of hawks—a hawkwatcher's identification challenge.

Most hawks can be categorized as either buteos, accipiters or falcons. **Buteos** are usu-

Red-tailed hawks are members of the buteos, or soaring hawks.

ally the most obvious, the quintessential hawk. Almost everyone has seen a red-tailed hawk, even if they did not know what it was, sitting on a fence post or a dead tree or perched along the interstate. Buteos are large, soaring hawks with long yet wide wings and fairly short tails. They generally prefer open country, prairie, meadow, marsh or croplands and feed largely on small rodents, reptiles and amphibians. Buteos hunt by watching for prey from a perch or by looking down as they soar high overhead, sometimes kiting (hanging motionless in the wind) or hovering (flapping in one spot). Prey is usually caught by surprise because the hawk spots it while unseen, far above.

Cooper's hawks, like all accipiters, are woodland raptors.

Accipiters are forest-dwelling hawks with short, rounded wings and long tails. This configuration suits their forest home. The long tail serves as a rudder aiding maneuverability as they pursue prey through and around trees and brush. Accipiters are often called bird hawks, feeding mostly on other birds that they catch in flight. Cooper's hawks and goshawks, however, frequently take chipmunks and squirrels. As woodland hawks, accipiters are comparatively rarely seen in either the breeding season or in winter. During migration, when they leave their forest homes behind, they are often seen in open country and along coastlines. This is the best time to spot accipiters. The smallest accipiter, the sharp-shinned hawk, is the hawk most likely to raid your bird feeder in winter.

Falcons differ considerably from other hawks. As a result, biologists place them in a separate family, the Falconidae. Falcons have long, pointed wings that are designed for rapid flight. They feed primarily on birds, but this is a generality. Merlins and kestrels take many insects, and the prairie falcon is a ground-squirrel specialist. Falcons are birds of open country—plains, prairies, marshes and tundra, and rarely enter woodlands. They chase down their prey with incredible speed, either in stoops or dogged tail chases.

A few hawks cannot be categorized as either buteos, accipiters or falcons. The **northern harrier** is a long-winged, long-tailed bird of open country—fields, prairies and marshes. There are many harrier species worldwide, but only one species is found in North America—the northern harrier, known to many as the marsh hawk. They hunt with low, coursing flight, and are highly maneuverable. The **osprey**, or fish hawk, is the most widely distributed raptor in the world. Ospreys are fish-eaters exclusively and differ from other raptors in having a reversible outer toe, an adaptation for catching and holding fish. Ospreys are large and boldly patterned, and capture fish by plunging into the water. The group of hawks known as **kites** exhibit a wide variety of shapes, color and behavior. Biologically, kites lack the bony ridge over the eye that all other hawks exhibit. The most common kites, the Mississippi kite and the white-tailed kite, resemble falcons, with long, pointed wings and tail. Kites hunt a variety of prey, from insects (Mississippi kite) to snails (hook-billed kite and snail kite).

Eagles are essentially very large hawks that

exhibit few behavioral or structural differences from buteos. While the largest buteo, the ferruginous hawk, has a wingspan up to 5 feet, an eagle's wingspan may reach 7½ feet. Bald eagles are opportunistic feeders, sometimes hunting or fishing, sometimes scavenging, and often pirating prey from other hawks, ospreys, ravens or gulls. Golden eagles are true hunters, taking mammalian and avian prey in dramatic dives and chases.

Finally, **vultures** differ considerably from all other groups of raptors. In fact, New World vultures differ widely from those found in the Old World; Western Hemisphere vultures are much more closely related to storks than to other birds of prey. Vultures have naked heads, weak feet and claws, and excellent eyesight. They are remarkably efficient at soaring; turkey vultures, while appearing "teetery," can tease lift from the lightest of winds or thermals. All vultures are scavengers, although the black vulture is rarely known to attack vulnerable, living prey. As such, vultures perform an important service as nature's clean-up crew.

Raptor Identification

IF SPOTTED CLOSE-BY or when sitting quietly in a tree or marsh, hawks can usually be classified first to type, then to species, using standard field identification marks. Most field guides point out the features that are unique to a particular species, such as the red shoulders of a red-shouldered hawk or the forked tail of a swallow-tailed kite. When such field marks are easily and clearly seen, identification can be straightforward. In using standard field marks, however, do not let the common names

of the birds confuse you. For instance, broad-winged hawks do not have particularly broad wings, and bald eagles certainly are not bald—the name refers to the white feathering on the head. (A far better name, and one which John James Audubon used, is "white-headed eagle.") You can only see the sharp keel on the legs of a sharp-shinned hawk when it is in your hand. Finally, while many (but not all) adult red-tailed hawks show bright reddish tails, other species show reddish tails as well (such as the male American kestrel), and young red-tails have brown, banded tails.

An important skill in spotting hawks and eagles is the ability to identify them in flight and in conditions that are often less than ideal: the bird may be seen only briefly, or at a great distance, or be backlit by the sun. Sometimes all of these adverse conditions occur at once, and standard field marks are not readily seen. In these situations, the observer must rely on the shape, silhouette, flight, patterns, movement and behavior of the bird. The overall shape and flight silhouette of a peregrine falcon, once learned, can be recognized from much farther away than a standard field mark like the facial pattern. The distinctive coursing flight of a harrier can be spotted at ten times the distance at which the "white rump" can be seen. Raptors are best identified using a holistic approach, which looks for the general impression, shape and size, or the "jizz" of the bird as it is referred to by birders. Most, if not all, of the distant identifications made at hawkwatches use this method.

When distinguishing between buteo, accipiter and falcon, it is important to remember that birds change shape depending on what

Hawks change shape in varying flight conditions. *Clockwise from top left:* **A red-tailed hawk in full soar; an open-winged glide; a fast, closed-wing glide; riding a strong updraft.**

they are doing. A soaring red-tail shows a classic buteo shape with wide wings, extended primaries and fanned tail. A gliding red-tail, however, has its wings pulled back, its primaries "closed," with the wings appearing pointed; the tail is closed and appears narrow, not fanned. When a red-tail is riding an updraft off a ridge in high winds, it is completely "folded up," with the outer wing pulled back parallel to the body. On one memorable day in November, we were watching red-tails with Pete Dunne on Raccoon Ridge in New Jersey in a 40-knot wind. The red-tails were going by "beak to tail" (a birdwatcher's term for

very frequently) looking like "flying cinder blocks," as Pete said, as they rode the updrafts off the ridge at point-blank range.

It is this variation in shape and appearance of an individual raptor that makes identification difficult. The key is to keep watching a given bird as it goes through changes in attitude. A gliding sharp-shin, which is not showing the watcher any identification points, will eventually begin soaring, revealing its characteristic accipiter shape. Never use just one field mark or trait; always go through a checklist of features when identifying a raptor.

Consider the type of habitat where you see

How to Spot Hawks & Eagles

a hawk or eagle to help make your identification. A bird dashing through the trees deep on a forest trail is not likely to be a falcon but probably is an accipiter—a forest-dwelling hawk. Conversely, a lone hawk perched on a telephone pole in farm country, miles from the nearest woods, is probably not an accipiter but is likely to be a buteo, most likely a red-tailed hawk. An eagle flying slowly over a marsh or lake is probably a bald eagle, due to their fishing habits and normal association with water. While habitat is normally a good key, remember that during migration, all bets are off. At that time, many birds appear outside of their normal haunts: accipiters may be far from forests, and falcons might be seen over (but not in) dense forests. At Cape May during the autumn migration, there is very little separation of species by habitat. We have often seen Cooper's hawks chasing flickers over the marsh, broad-winged hawks perched in hedgerows, even peregrines perched on telephone poles in town. During spring migration near Laguna Atascosa National Wildlife Refuge in Texas, we saw numerous ospreys perched in open farm fields, far from water.

Range Clues

THE NORMAL RANGE of a raptor species is important information. Frequently you can use it to make an identification by the process of elimination. Once you have determined the type and size of the hawk, check the range maps in your field guide. A dark buteo on the mid-Atlantic coast in winter is not a zone-tailed hawk, because they are only found in the Southwest. It is not a Swainson's hawk, be-

cause their wintering grounds are in Argentina. Odds are the bird is a dark-form rough-legged hawk.

Understanding the timing of raptor migration and likely routes they follow gives you other important clues. Many species can be eliminated from consideration by knowing when they are most likely to migrate. A large, dark falcon on the New England coast in November may well be not a peregrine but a gyrfalcon; and a rangy "falcon" on the southern Atlantic Coast in early June will probably not be a peregrine either but more likely the remarkably similar-appearing Mississippi kite. A band-tailed buteo at Derby Hill, New York, in early March is unlikely to be a broadwinged hawk, since they are just beginning to pour north over the Panama Canal Zone on their long journey back home.

What to expect (according to breeding range and migration routes) and when to expect it (knowing the proper migration season) can be invaluable in making an identification. And for the birder looking for specific species, this knowledge is critical. If you have never seen peregrines and wish to see them in good numbers, a journey to Cape May in the first week of October would be ideal—but a trip during the first week of September or in November might not yield even one sighting. For anyone wishing to see a golden eagle, or many goldens, Hawk Mountain Sanctuary during the first few days of November is a must. For broad-wings, a trip to the Texas coast or to the Santa Ana National Wildlife Refuge (NWR) in the last week of March or the first week of April will almost guarantee you a window on their migration spectacle at its best.

Finding Raptors

SOUTH TEXAS during the first week of April is normally hot. This is when the "snowbirds," the retirees, are leaving, escaping the growing southern heat and heading home to points north. For three days though, the skies over the Rio Grande Valley had been leaden, with rain coming on a bitter northeast wind. We each wore sweaters and sweatshirts, wishing for our down jackets left behind back home.

The hawks were there though—several thousand broad-wings had been stranded in the oasis of lush habitat that is Santa Ana NWR. As we walked the trails pursuing least grebes and buff-bellied hummingbirds, hawks constantly flushed ahead of us—making us feel guilty of bird harassment. Santa Ana is magnificent, but 4,000 acres is not enough habitat to support thousands of hawks for long. There are only so many frogs, insects and mice available, and any still uncaught were certainly hawk-wise by now.

The restlessness of the broad-wings was obvious. Each morning they would try to circle up into the low clouds and gray skies, skies which offered little of the much-sought-after lift. And each morning, just as they began to disappear to the north of the refuge, the hawks would begin flapping back in, their proverbial tails between their legs. They needed to move. Little food was available, migratory fat was diminishing, and the northern forests and breeding season beckoned. In late afternoon in the gathering gloom, a plaintive whistle came from a nearby perched broad-wing, possibly think-

The Santa Ana National Wildlife Refuge, in Texas, is an excellent site for observing spring concentrations of broad-winged hawks, such as the one at *right*.

How to Spot Hawks & Eagles

ing of his home woodlot somewhere in Ontario, Maine or Vermont.

On the fourth morning, the wind switched to the southeast—not a tail wind but close enough—and the skies began to clear. Hawks began to rise, even before the thermals formed. As the sun broke through and the forests of Santa Ana warmed, the sky over the refuge began to fill with hawks, wheeling masses of broad-wings. The kettles were scattered and low at first, but gradually began to ascend and coalesce. Soon boiling masses of hawks dominated the view over the refuge. Forty here, 200 there, 80 beyond. Only then did we realize the numbers of raptors the riparian forests of the Rio Grande had been hiding.

We were on the flood-control dike overlooking the refuge. As the sky opened up and sunlight flooded through, sunglasses, visors and sunscreen became the order of the day. Sweatshirt soon gave way to sweater, sweater to flannel shirt, flannel shirt to T-shirt. Warmth flooded the valley. The unexpected numbers of "stranded" hawks soon formed into magnificent kettles of 400 and 500 birds apiece. They did not linger. At an altitude at which they were disappearing to the naked eye, yet still spectacular in binoculars, they peeled off and began streaming north, heading home to their natal forests.

There was a lull as the "locals" disappeared, but soon our spotting scopes revealed hundreds, no *thousands* of hawks kettling to the south, well out beyond the Rio Grande River. Soon these birds were streaming overhead, a river of raptors coming out of Mexico, heading north with the spring. The next several hours were ranked among the finest experience a hawkwatcher can have. Soon Swainson's hawks began to appear among the broad-wings, first a few mixed in, then a pure Swainson's hawk kettle of about 50 birds. High beyond the swirling buteos came a stream of hundreds of turkey vultures surging north. There was some variety: Cooper's hawks were always in sight, and kestrels were constantly pumping through. The first Mississippi kites of the season appeared high against the boiling clouds, heading for Kansas shelterbelts.

Just as the flight peaked, an adult gray hawk briefly circled with the broad-wings. As if spurred by all the activity, the resident hook-billed kites finally appeared (we had been looking for them in vain for three days), weaving in and out of the broad-winged hawk kettles in spirited courtship flights. By 11 A.M., it seemed over, but by using spotting scopes against the few remaining clouds, we could pick out tiny specks streaming over—broad-wings and Swainson's at the limit of aided vision—at heights only a veteran raptor enthusiast could appreciate.

Our Santa Ana morning had been hawk-watching at its best. This Rio Grande Valley flight occurs on some variation of the above script every spring and fall. The last week of March and first ten days of April are when the major spring push occurs for broad-wings. The fall peak takes place during the period from September 18 to about October 6. What we had witnessed was just one example of how planning and preparation can provide the opportunity for a truly memorable spotting experience.

How to Look

As Jack Connor explained in *The Complete Birder*: "One problem is that hawk-watching requires a different technique from other forms of birdwatching. Most field and woodland birding is stalk and stab. You walk quietly and, when you come upon a bird, snap your binoculars to your eyes for a quick look. The drama is played out in a few moments, and you either get the bird or you don't. Hawkwatching, especially at lookout sites, is more like reeling in a fish. A raptor appears off in the distance, swimming in the sky. You must find the bird in your binocs and then hang onto it—for a long, slow, wrist-trembling, neck-crinking, eye-straining diagnosis. If you keep at it long enough and you're lucky, you may pull the bird in close enough for its field marks to become obvious. More often, the hawk breaks away by dropping below the trees or soaring into the sun."

In most types of birding the watcher looks for movement and color or listens for calls. These strategies are of limited use in searching for hawks, which may be above the horizon or perched motionless on a distant fence post. With raptors, generally, you must search actively with your binoculars. They don't present themselves to you as songbirds often do. Scan treelines, hedgerows and dead trees looking for perched raptors. In the tree-poor prairie states or in agricultural areas, hawks often perch on fence posts, utility poles, windmills or even oil rigs. These may offer the only elevated perches around for hunting views. Transmission-line towers often hold raptors as well. Large vulture roosts sometimes form on the crossbars of these towers. Perched raptors will usually be silhouetted against the sky or distant landscape. Against darker foliage, the light breasts of many hawks will stand out.

Use your binoculars to scan above the tree-tops or above the horizon to spot flying raptors. For distant birds, try a scan that keeps the treetops in the very bottom of your binocular field. Be sure to set the focus wheel on infinity. Scan ridgetops where raptors may be getting lift off the cliff face. You must also

Actively use your binoculars to search for hawks: scan treelines, horizons, ridgetops and the sky.

scan the sky overhead. When clouds are present, scan across and around the clouds. Hawks, even when just "specks in the sky" are easier to pick out when they are against a cloud. At established hawkwatches, where it is important to count every hawk, counters will search the blue sky in a grid pattern, scanning up from the ground all the way to overhead, doing this every few points of the compass in the direction from which the expected flight is coming.

Even if you are at an organized hawkwatch, with many people around, it is much more fun to use your binoculars and scan for new birds than to wait for someone else to find the next hawk. Scan for distant specks. Are they crows? Are they gulls? Or are they the eagerly awaited migrating raptors?

Remember that practice pays off: the more hawks you spot and attempt to recognize, the better your identification skills will become. Compare your ID on the bird with that of the official counter, or with other watchers present. Slowly the process will fall into place. The best birders are the ones who consistently try to identify every bird they see.

Finding a distant bird may lead to an even better spotting opportunity. If you can drive or hike closer to a perched raptor, you may discover more than one. At Sonoita Creek, Arizona, we watched a distant zone-tailed hawk quartering back and forth over the trees. Taking a nearby road behind the riparian forest, we moved to a place where we could see a second zone-tailed hawk join the first over the trees. Soon we heard calls—they were coming from a nest in the trees above us. Much to our delight, there were two young zone-tails in it. We spent the next hour watching the adults come and go and the young testing their wings, possibly for the first time, above their cottonwood home.

Equipment and Techniques

SPOTTING HAWKS AND EAGLES does not require a great deal of equipment. The optics recommended for general birding will suffice for hawkwatching. As in most birding, good binoculars are a must—a clean pair with good light-gathering ability that are in precise alignment—not a pair that your son dropped down the front stairs or a pair that Uncle Harry brought back from the Second World War. If you have not had the occasion to use state-of-the-art binoculars recently, you may be astounded at the clarity of today's models—even low- to middle-priced ones.

Binocular quality really makes a difference. At a good hawkwatch, during a good migration, you may use your binoculars more in one day than a casual birder uses them in a year. Focusing on a distant bird against a featureless sky will quickly tell you if your binoculars are out of alignment—something that may not be apparent when using them in the woods. As field trip leaders, we often hear the lament, "I don't see that on the bird," or "It doesn't look reddish to me." Looking through their binoculars, we can't see that feature either, or can't see the reddish coloration. Simply put, the inferior binoculars are not up to the job. If you are serious about raptor watching, invest in a good pair of binoculars. With proper care, they will last a lifetime. They are your link to the world of hawks and eagles.

The best binoculars for hawkwatching are quality 7x (7-power), 8x, or 10x models, with a good twilight or light-gathering capability.

Even at an established hawkwatch, such as this one at Cape May, New Jersey, it is much more rewarding to scan for new birds than to wait for someone else to spot one for you.

Magnification, usually called "power," determines how close an object will appear and what details will be seen. In 7x42 binoculars, the first number stands for the power of magnification: 7x binoculars will bring an object seven times closer to the viewer and make it appear that many times larger. A hawk 1,400 feet away will thus appear to be only 200 feet away. Brightness is also a critical variable in selecting binoculars. The amount of light a binocular draws in depends largely on the size of the front (objective) lenses, and is denoted by the number following the multiplication sign. In 7x42 binoculars, the 42 indicates the size of the objective lens in millimeters. The larger the objective lens, the greater its light-gathering capability. While many birders talk about the "light-gathering factor" or "relative light efficiency" of binoculars, formulas to determine this are somewhat meaningless and rarely straightforward, due to varying degrees of optical coating and ongoing advances in the methods and types of coatings. The more expensive binoculars utilize the best coatings to allow the most light transfer. A final factor to consider in binoculars is the field of view, the amount of area that will be visible edge to edge. Because hawkwatching involves a lot of scanning, wide-angle binoculars are best.

For an in-depth explanation of binoculars, we highly recommend reading the "Optics" chapter in Jack Connor's *The Complete Birder*. But the bottom line is that you need not be overly concerned with the technical aspects of binoculars—a top brand should be more than up to the task. If you have the opportunity, attend an optics workshop. Pete Dunne teaches them regularly for the Cape May Bird Observatory. Hawk Mountain in Pennsylvania has visiting optics company representatives available on different weekends to answer questions. During such workshops, you have a chance to learn from a birder or naturalist, ask questions and compare a number of brands in varying price ranges. Nature center bookstores that carry a good selection of optics give you the chance to see what feels best around your neck, in your hands and to your eyes.

Absolutely avoid fixed-focus models or instant focus models. These are gimmicks—veteran birders unanimously prefer the crisp focusing ability that comes from the "old-fashioned" focusing wheel. Resist the urge for powers higher than 10. When Clay started hawkwatching, he used 7x binoculars but soon moved up to instant-focus 10x. Then, he reasoned, if 10x's are good, why not try 20x? The 20x's lasted less than one year before he went back to 10x (this time to a name brand) and ultimately back to Zeiss 7x42. The extra power was simply not worth the extra weight and the added wobble (vibration) in the image. The main problems with the 20x were lack of light, darkness of the image and lack of color. While Clay was looking at dark images of hawks, albeit larger ones, others were enjoying crystal-clear views, picking up much more color and detail.

Many feel that the Zeiss 10x40 is one of the best binoculars for hawkwatching. We both used them for many years, although we now use Zeiss 7x42, probably a better all-around birding binocular. Others in the same class as Zeiss are the Bausch & Lomb Elite 8x42, the Leica 10x42, and the Swarovski 7x42 and 10x42. The new Nikon porro-prism 10x42 and Leica 10x50 are also excellent and could be the new hawkwatching binoculars against which all others are measured. Expect to pay about $1,000 for any of these state-of-the-art, high-quality binoculars. An excellent mid-price-range binocular is the venerable Swift 8.5x44 Audubon model (about $300), which measures up very well against the more expensive models. These Swifts are particularly popular with eyeglass wearers. Mirador and Bausch and Lomb also make good mid-priced binoculars. If you plan extensive hawkwatching, we recommend you don't go any lower in price. If you do, you will eventually feel the need to upgrade. To rationalize the cost, remember that your binoculars are a lifetime investment and one of the few expenses your hobby requires.

If you desire more power and closer views, carry a spotting scope. There are many hawk and eagle spotting situations where such a scope is advantageous. Again, buy a state-of-the-art scope. Astronomy-type telescopes do not work in the field because of their high power, narrow field of view, and bulk. You will want a field-model scope, one designed specifically for birding. Most birders avoid zoom scopes. Zoom optics (including binoculars) are a compromise; optical quality is never as good as with fixed eyepieces. For viewing raptors, it is best to carry two spotting-scope eyepieces. A wide-angle eyepiece of 20x, 22x or 30x will allow you to scan extensively for perched hawks, and you can even locate and follow soaring birds. Many European hawkwatchers prefer 45-degree-angle eyepieces.

They allow for a much more comfortable stance while scanning and seem to partially eliminate eye fatigue ("scope eye") by providing a dark, out-of-focus background (the ground) for the other eye. The second (and less important) eyepiece should be anywhere between 40x and 60x. There will be some days (or times of day) when there will be either not enough light, too many heat waves or too much wind (vibration) to use the higher power, but other bright, clear days will allow you to use the high-power eyepiece to the best advantage. The lower-power, wide-angle eyepiece will receive, by far, the most use in hawkwatching.

The Bushnell Spacemaster II has been a workhorse for many years now, and this scope with the 22x wide-angle eyepiece is a journeyman optic that is hard to beat. Many today believe the Kowa TSN-4 to be the state-of-the-art scope (specify the 30x wide-angle eyepiece), but Optolyth, Swarovski and Nikon all have models that are the Kowa's equal. Expect to pay about $250 for the Bushnell with eyepiece, and around $1,120 for the Kowa TSN-4 with 30x eyepiece. Many birders feel that the Kowa TSN-2 performs every bit as well as the TSN-4, at about half the price. The major difference in performance seems to be in very low light conditions, not usually a factor in most raptor spotting.

Do not make the mistake of putting an expensive spotting scope on a cheap, flimsy tripod. The best scope in the world is of little value if the image is bobbing or vibrating so much that you cannot enjoy it. A good-quality, sturdy tripod is as important as the scope itself. There is a weight penalty—a steady image requires a hefty tripod—but it is a penalty worth paying. Backpacks specifically designed to carry spotting scopes and tripods are now available, advertised in most birding maga-

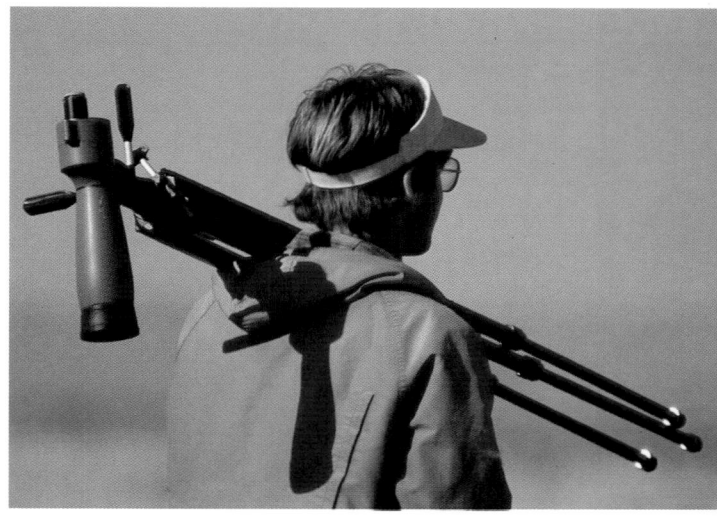

A good spotting scope and a sturdy tripod are a must for raptor watching, Sun visors are invaluable for blocking glare when scanning the skies.

zines or available in nature center stores. These will help transport your scope to distant hawk and eagle viewing areas. When you purchase a tripod, specify a fluid head for ease of panning. Many birders have their own favorite tripods, but after having a number of different tripods fall apart on us, we can strongly state that Bogen tripods, such as their model 3122, are the best available today. Expect to pay around $150 for a Bogen tripod with a fluid head. Finally, a window mount for your scope will allow you to search for raptors from your car on bitter winter days. Actually, using your car as a blind can often allow a close approach to perched raptors. Driving back roads in open areas is an excellent way to spot hawks, then use your window-mounted scope to get a closer view. We know a number of birders who use quick-release mechanisms to switch their scopes from tripod to window mount. This avoids the constant unscrewing and screwing when switching. Ask about these when you purchase a window mount.

For established watches at hawk migration hotspots, a few other items of equipment can be extremely useful. Sunglasses are important for looking into bright skies for migrating birds, and a baseball cap or visor helps block the sun's glare. Needless to say, sunscreen can be critical for anyone spending a full day staring at the sky. Many veteran hawkwatchers bring folding chairs to lookouts. If you plan to spend a few hours "waiting for the eagle," a chair can make your stay far more comfortable. Folding camp stools or lightweight chairs that can be easily carried and fit in your car trunk are ideal. We know one person who brings a folding chaise recliner to the Cape May hawkwatch, all the better for spotting high-flying "speck" raptors. Others bring a blanket. Lying down and staring straight up can be an excellent way to watch hawks overhead without incurring lower back or neck pain. (There are those who say that Ben-Gay is essential equipment for prolonged hawk viewing.)

Warm clothes can also be essential. Watching peregrines streaking over Big Pine Key, Florida, in October may not call for anything more than a bathing suit, but we guarantee that watching a rough-legged hawk flight at Braddock Bay, New York, in early March will require the warmest clothes (and boots) made. One of the coldest days we ever spent hawkwatching (or anywhere) was in November at Raccoon Ridge on the Kittatinny Mountains, in New Jersey. Bundled in parkas, we hid behind rock pinnacles to stay out of the wind as best we could under somber skies with snow flurries. Cold, yes, but the 400 plus red-tails, 7 golden eagles, 5 bald eagles, and several goshawks made the frigid vigil well worth it. For such outings, we recommend winter parkas and/or a down jacket, long underwear, wool gloves, a wool watch cap, warm winter boots and wool socks. We prefer boots with waterproof rubber bottoms, leather tops and thick wool liners that wrap the foot and ankle in insulating warmth. If the feet or the hands grow cold, so does your enthusiasm. As Clay's grandfather always said, "If you're too warm, you can take it off, but if you don't have it with you, you can't put it on."

Active Searching

SPOTTING HAWKS AND EAGLES requires more search techniques than does general birding. In everyday birding, one usually responds to bird song, color or movement in grass, bushes or trees. To find hawks you must search actively—but not randomly. Experienced hawkwatchers use tricks to locate distant perched or high flying raptors, techniques that help filter birds from seemingly empty landscapes and skies.

If initially you find a few hawks perched, there are probably no thermals or "flight conditions," and most if not all raptors will be

During migration flights, broad-wings form flocks, or "kettles," in rising columns of warm air.

altitude. At midday, concentrate your searching overhead, for this is when hawks can be at considerable altitude. Scan the sky and cloud formations. If cumulus clouds are forming, check them with your binoculars. Cumulus clouds usually indicate the presence and location of thermals, rising columns of warmer air that soaring birds seek to gain lift. Hawks are much more easily seen as silhouettes against the white background of clouds than against a clear blue sky.

Once you find a raptor, keep an eye on it. Remember, birds of a feather *do* flock together. Most raptors have a tendency to form flocks, if only because they all want to be in the best thermals. Scan around the sky in the area of your bird. Large, dark birds, like eagles and vultures, are much easier to pick out than smaller, pale-bellied birds. If you find a group of vultures, do not dismiss them. Keep watching to see if other raptors join them in the kettle. During migration, this happens frequently. Vultures will generally indicate where the best thermals are, and mixed-species kettles quickly form.

perched. This is the time to scan exposed perches, first with your binoculars, then with your scope. In bad weather, hawks, like most birds, attempt to get out of the wind, rain or snow. At times like this, look on the lee side of ridges, woods and hedgerows. In winter in the Northeast, red-shouldered hawks are often found in early morning perched on sunny edges and out of the wind; they are probably warming up as much as they are hunting. This behavior is so dependable that we always search for them in such situations during Christmas Bird Counts.

If you find one raptor soaring, probably most raptors will be doing the same, taking advantage of good thermals. In general, early in the morning and late in the day are the times to scan just above the horizon. At these times the sun is low, thermals are minimal, there is little lift, and birds will not have much

If the hawk you find is gliding, scan the flight path both ahead of and behind the bird—birds usually follow each other from one thermal to the next. At migration points, ospreys and harriers usually come in twos and threes or even in much larger groups. At Cape May, we have seen "streams" of up to 12 ospreys on the same flight line, one behind the other. Also we have seen up to nine harriers together taking the same flight path. American kestrels almost always travel in loose groups. Early in the season, small family groups travel together. Later, during peak migration, small waves migrate together, often up to eight or ten birds at a time.

At migration junctures, you can often see specific flight lines develop. At some sites, there are established flight paths governed by geography and wind direction. Once you note one bird's course, you can usually find others following the same path, as long as conditions (wind direction and speed) do not change. This is how some birders make most or all of the good finds at a hawkwatch. It is not that their eyes or binoculars are necessarily superior, but that they have learned the "conditions" and know where to look. At Hawk Mountain, I have seen every eagle of the day appear in exactly the same place over "Number 2" peak, coming straight in on the same flight line. Different wind conditions may shift the flight anywhere from the "Pinnacle" to "Number 5." At Cape May, we have seen nine bald eagles appear in succession over "the pole" (a former radio tower) on north winds. Let the wind switch to the northwest, though, and these birds will usually appear over the town of Cape May. If the wind goes northeast, the flight line usually shifts to "over the Magnesite Plant" (a section of the skyline that will always be called that even though the factory was demolished years ago). You do not need to know a site well to figure out the flight lines. Carefully observe where raptors first appear and the path they are taking. Then continue to do the bulk (but not all) of your scanning in that sec-

tor of the sky. Also, it helps to learn the topography at any new watch site, so that when a fellow watcher calls out "rough-leg over the High Point tower," you know exactly where to look.

Telltale Indicators

THERE ARE A NUMBER of other clues used by veteran hawkwatchers. Remember that raptors are predators. To find predators, you need to find prey. If you concentrate your birding around aggregations of prey species, sooner or later, probably sooner, raptors will show up. Shorebird concentrations on mudflats, bays or inlets often attract peregrines and merlins. Gatherings of sparrows along woodland edges and hedgerows are sure bets to attract sharp-shinned hawks and Cooper's hawks, particularly in fall and winter. Giant blackbird flocks may attract anything from merlins to red-tailed hawks. Bald eagles often gravitate to feeding flocks of gulls on marshes, lakes and rivers. The eagles may be interested in whatever the gulls are feeding on, or possibly in the gulls themselves. In winter, crows and ravens feeding on carrion such as a deer carcass are sure to attract eagles and even red-tailed hawks and rough-legged hawks. Waterfowl flocks attract eagles, both bald and golden, that often haze the flock to single out stragglers or injured birds. In winter, freeze-ups on lakes and rivers are an extremely good way to find eagles, which are attracted to winter-stressed waterfowl and winter-killed fish.

Once you have found prey, there are a number of hints you can use for finding the associated raptors. Many times we have found high-flying hawks after seeing birds on the ground cock their heads to look up. Since they have more of a vested interest than we do, prey species usually know if a raptor is overhead. If you see shorebirds pause to look skyward, follow their gaze. Likewise, if you are studying a perched raptor and it cocks its head to look up, trace its line of sight—you will probably spot a high-flying raptor. If birds suddenly freeze and remain motionless for some time, it is a sure clue that a raptor is about. Many times, we have seen this happen at our feeder and have looked up to see a circling sharp-shinned hawk. If your normally busy bird feeder is inexplicably deserted, no doubt an accipiter is nearby.

The calls of songbirds can also be a spotting signal. Almost every day at our bird feeder, the high, thin alarm note of the Carolina chickadee alerts us to the presence of a raptor, usually a sharp-shinned hawk. Learn the "blink" alarm call of the starling, a sure indicator of a nearby raptor. Jays are also excellent hawk finders once you become familiar with their alarm calls.

The mobbing behavior and agitated calls of crows always mean that they have located a raptor, either an owl, a hawk or an eagle. Crows particularly like to pick on bald eagles and goshawks. The appearance of a whirling, turning ball or tight flock of starlings indicates that a hawk is close by in the sky. Flocking behavior or "balling-up" is similar to mobbing, although balled-up birds make no effort to attack the hawk. They appear to circle above the raptor, much as a school of fish might close up for safety, in order to keep the raptor in sight and keep it from singling out one target.

To find raptors, first find prey. In the West, prairie dog colonies, *top*, attract red-tails, ferruginous hawks and golden eagles. A shorebird pausing to look skyward, such as this sanderling, *bottom*, may indicate the presence of a raptor overhead.

We have seen tree swallow flocks form a tight ball when a merlin appears, making them less vulnerable to attack. Wheeling, twisting flocks of shorebirds over a mudflat usually indicate the presence of a falcon, either a merlin or a peregrine. Pigeons can be good raptor spotters as well, flushing and circling until the threat passes. Balling-up is visible at a great distance and is an excellent spotting clue.

A red-tailed hawk may call because it is upset by your presence, but it may also indicate another interloper nearby. The whistling call of an osprey high overhead usually means one of two things. Either another osprey is nearby, or that veteran fish pirate, the bald eagle, is in the same air space. If an osprey is calling, find out why.

Always be alert for any spontaneous flushing that is not man-related. Songbirds flushing wildly all at once probably means an accipiter attack. Waterfowl flushing can be a dead giveaway of a raptor's location. Ducks will often (but not always) flush at the approach of an eagle—we once watched the progress of an eagle down the Merrimac River

in Massachusetts, preceded by clouds of waterfowl rising up. At Forsythe (Brigantine) National Wildlife Refuge (NWR) in New Jersey, we have seen a peregrine's progress across the impoundments heralded by a rising wave of green-winged teal. Snow geese can be good indicators of an oncoming eagle. We have charted an eagle's movement over a marsh by rising clamorous clouds of snow geese in such diverse areas as Squaw Creek NWR in Missouri and Blackwater NWR in Maryland on the Chesapeake Bay.

Gulls can be good spotters of raptors as well. In coastal, river or lake regions, the simultaneous flushing of flocks of gulls will always reveal the presence of an eagle. At Cape May, where gulls are somewhat inured to raptors, usually only an eagle or sometimes a peregrine will flush them, although we have seen them fooled by black vultures and red-tailed hawks. Hundreds of eagles have been spotted over the years at Cape May by watchers who have searched after being alerted by flushing gulls. If the gulls settle back down right away, it was a false alarm, probably man- or dog-related, but if they all circle tightly, high overhead, wheeling and calling in a towering flock, you can rely on this as the unmistakable sign of an eagle's presence. Do not necessarily expect to find it overhead immediately—it may yet be a mile or so out or too high to be seen—but you can be sure it is there.

Waterfowl wildly flushing (suddenly taking wing) can be a telltale sign of an eagle approaching overhead.

How to Spot Hawks & Eagles

Where to Look

CERTAINLY EVERY BIT as important as knowing how to look for hawks and eagles is knowing where to look. Open space is the key, and most areas where some natural open space is found hold some raptors, at least in season. The size of available habitat is important. As predators, raptors usually require large territories, during both the breeding and winter seasons. While sparsely vegetated suburban lots are probably not large enough to provide hawks with their food and cover needs, corridors and greenbelts, even in urban areas, may well be adequate, particularly during migration periods.

Some hawks have adapted quite well to urban environments. The success of peregrine falcons in colonizing city landscapes, where they nest on high-rise buildings or skyscrapers and feed on pigeons, is well known. Less well known is how adapted some other raptor species are to urban situations. American kestrels can do quite well as long as some grassy meadows or farmlands are available nearby. In New Jersey, we have watched kestrels nesting under hotel eaves in Glassboro and Cape May City. Red-tailed hawks have nested in Fairmount Park in the heart of Philadelphia. Cooper's hawks, once thought to be exclusively birds of wild areas, have adjusted to suburban habitats where an abundance of pigeons and starlings are present as food. In winter, there are few places in North America (south of heavy snow cover) where sharp-shinned hawks do not regularly raid bird feeders. With well-stocked bird feeders and good-sized flocks of house sparrows and house finches, it can be hard not to attract a wintering sharp-shinned hawk or two. In this case, you can spot a hawk in your own backyard. While some people are upset at the prospect of a hawk taking songbirds, for others, the sharp-shinned or Cooper's hawk at their feeder is the "best bird" of the winter and a chance to watch the process of natural selection at work. Be alert though, since raids can be bold and brief. Often the presence of the hawk is only detected by the flushing or freezing behavior of the songbirds.

Once ample open space is found, vistas are important. Although many raptors live in forests, you are far more likely to see them from an overlook with an open view than you are while walking in deep, unbroken forest. If hiking in wooded regions, stop at openings, overlooks, blowdowns or edges to scan horizon and sky.

Suitable Habitats

HABITAT PREFERENCE varies by type of raptor and by species. In general, accipiters prefer forest areas, using them extensively if not exclusively during the breeding season. In winter, they might be found in a variety of habitats. To find buteos, scan open country—prairies, meadows and farmland. Although red-shouldered hawks and broad-winged hawks are forest dwellers during the breeding season, they are best spotted by scanning forest edges and treelines from adjacent overlooks. Transmission-line rights-of-way provide excellent access to raptor habitat—they often cut through vast forests and offer views of the sky and horizon. On one memo-

In both the nesting season and in winter, bald eagles concentrate along rivers, lakes, reservoirs and seacoasts, because fish make up such a large portion of their diet.

rable walk along a right-of-way in the mountainous New Jersey Highlands, we spotted a family of red-shoulders, a pair of broad-wings, a goshawk carrying prey to its unseen nest, and an adult Cooper's hawk—not to mention a black bear. Abandoned railroad lines can serve the same purpose as transmission lines; we have used them extensively in lowland areas for access to and views of wooded regions.

Open country is definitely a requirement for spotting falcons. Scan marshes, prairies, meadows and tundra. Coastal areas are excellent. Beaches, bays and inlets are good for peregrines and merlins during migration.

River valleys and lakeshores produce many sightings. Prairie falcons can be found in fairly arid areas, but grasslands are best. In the flatlands of the West, bluffs, cliffs and buttes can be magnets for falcons. Canyon walls attract nesting falcons.

Eagles are often portrayed as birds of remote mountain regions, and this is certainly valid. Golden eagles particularly prefer inaccessible or unapproachable mountain ridges and valleys during the nesting season, but can be found well away from these areas in winter. In the southwest, golden eagles are often spotted along prairie or cattleland roadsides.

Scan transmission-line poles and fence posts to find perched birds.

Bald eagles can be found in some mountainous areas, but only if extensive lakes are present—they are essentially birds of watery areas, probably because fish comprise such a large portion of their diet. In both the nesting season and in winter, bald eagles concentrate along rivers, lakes, reservoirs and seacoasts. Marshes and remote inlets are likely choices also. These stately birds often perch low. Scan river edges, islands, ice flows, muskrat houses, beaver lodges and duck blinds to find motionless, perched birds. Be alert; they can blend into the background amazingly well. At Squaw Creek NWR in Missouri, we saw 87 bald eagles perched on the ice and on muskrat houses on an early January morning. At Blackwater NWR in Maryland, 16 immature bald eagles were chasing one another and perching on the tidal mudflats at first light on a bitter cold February morning. In the Everglades on Florida Bay, bald eagles can sometimes be seen sitting on the mudflats in the bright, shimmering tropical spring light.

While finding hawks and eagles does not require remote wilderness areas, getting away from people and traffic can definitely improve your chances and views. In Florida, for example, many dozens of raptors of many species can be seen from Interstate 95 or from the Florida Turnpike, but views can be less than satisfying with traffic whizzing by. Instead, take parallel roads, the roads less traveled. Look for parks and wildlife areas along the route. For example, Three Lakes Wildlife Management Area, just off the Florida Turnpike, provides quiet views of crested caracaras

and bald eagles. In Texas, in winter, hundreds of hawks can be seen along Route 77 south of Corpus Christi, but it is all viewing from the side of a busy highway. Instead, take the various farm roads around Kingsville to get off the beaten path. By traveling on these secondary roads, you can usually find good overviews and close-up looks at hawks. Remember to pull well off the road so you do not block the occasional traffic. And *never* trespass—not even for "just one photograph."

As a general rule, the more rural the route, the better your chances of having a close raptor encounter.

Public Lands

ONE SURE WAY TO FIND RAPTORS is to frequent known raptor-concentration areas. Raptors are attracted by quality habitat and good concentrations of prey. The U.S. Fish and Wildlife Service National Wildlife Refuge system administers nearly 400 national wildlife refuges nationwide. While few are set aside primarily for raptors, all provide excellent habitat for many species of birds—waterfowl, shorebirds and songbirds—and raptors are amply attracted as well. We have watched bald eagles at Parker River NWR in Massachusetts and seen scores of northern harriers and peregrines in a day at Pea Island NWR in North Carolina. Swallow-tailed kites have entertained us at Lake Woodruff NWR and snail kites at Loxahatchee NWR in Florida. In the Midwest, we have seen kettles of bald eagles and a dozen Harlan's (red-tailed) hawks on December days at Squaw Creek NWR in Missouri. We have had excellent success on winter and spring trips to Quivira NWR in Kansas, and Oklahoma's many refuges (Salt Plains, Washita, Sequoyah, Wichita Mountains, and Tishomingo) have given us opportunity to study all the varied plumages of red-tails, as well as ferruginous hawks and prairie falcons. Muleshoe NWR in Texas is great for ferruginous hawks, along with tens of thousands of sandhill cranes in winter. Laguna Atascosa NWR in Texas is a premier refuge, with the largest bird list of any refuge in the nation, including white-tailed hawks, Harris' hawks, white-tailed kites and aplomado falcons. In California, golden eagles and Swainson's hawks have excited us at Kern NWR, and we recall a memorable sky dance by harriers over San Francisco Bay NWR. All this and we have only scratched the surface of the National Wildlife Refuge system. We have never been disappointed. All hold rap-tors, many at every season, and each visit is an adventure. With so many refuges nation-wide, one is likely to be near you. Plan a visit. Most refuges have offices and can provide information both on raptors and on other refuges within the system. *A Guide to the National Wildlife Refuges, How to Get There, What to See and Do*, by Laura and William Riley, is a comprehensive overview and gives details on many raptor opportunities.

On a state level, most Wildlife Areas, Wildlife Management Areas or State Game-lands (titles vary from state to state) provide suitable places to observe raptors. They function in much the same way as national wildlife refuges, providing habitat and cover for many species of wildlife, but usually (although not always) on a smaller scale. For example, Mac-Namara Wildlife Management Area (WMA) is one of the best places in New Jersey to see rough-legged hawks and golden eagles in winter, and osprey and harriers nest there in summer. The Santee Delta Wildlife Area and the Santee Coastal Reserve in South Carolina are two of our favorite swallow-tailed and Mississippi kite-watching areas in spring and summer. To learn more about state wildlife lands, contact your state wildlife agencies. Be sure to ask about access (some are closed in the off-season) and about hunting seasons, since nearly all these wildlife areas are heavily used during hunting season.

In addition, our national parks, national forests and national grasslands are excellent for birding and all have raptors in residence. We have been thrilled

Search the plantations of the South Carolina low country for swallow-tailed and Mississippi kites. The Santee River area is an ideal site.

How to Spot Hawks & Eagles

The more remote the area, the better your chance of spotting a golden eagle like this adult.

by goshawks riding the updrafts off the walls of the Grand Canyon, watched Mississippi and swallow-tailed kites cavorting in the boiling cumulus summer thermals over Francis Marion National Forest in South Carolina, and spotted hundreds of kestrels and merlins skimming the coastal dunes during their spring migration at Sandy Hook, New Jersey, in the Gateway National Recreation Area. Prairie falcons and Swainson's hawks have entertained us in the late-spring skies over the vastness of Pawnee National Grassland in Colorado. In our finest raptor moment, on a misty, melancholy April day in 1978, we watched 12 California condors soaring in unison over Los Padres National Forest in California, the last ballet of the giants, before they were removed from the wild for captive breeding in a desperate effort to stave off extinction.

Public lands also provide some of the best places in Canada to find raptors. One of our most memorable golden eagle spottings was of a pair soaring over wilderness alpine meadows above treeline in Jasper National Park. Ironically, both the eagles and we were doing the same thing—looking for white-tailed ptarmigans.

Point Pelee National Park, on the north shore of Lake Erie in Ontario, is one of the best hawkwatching spots on the continent in the fall. Here, hawks mistake the Point for what they hope is a land bridge across the lake, and pile up in large numbers at the end. Farther west, the autumn hawk flights at Holiday Beach Conservation Area are legendary: southbound hawks and eagles trapped on the north side of Lake Ontario and then Lake Erie (remember, hawks do not like to fly over water) are concentrated in enormous numbers prior to their passing south into the United States. These are only a few examples of the raptor-watching possibilities in Canadian public open spaces.

We've enjoyed Swainson's hawks, such as this one, on the prairies in spring at Colorado's Pawnee National Grassland.

Bird Finding Guides

THERE ARE MANY SITE GUIDES now available to good birding areas, and most highlight worthwhile hawkwatching spots. Foremost among these guides are the ABA/Lane Guides (see Further Information, page 131). The watching instructions are wonderfully specific: "Another interesting spot is 6.8 miles past the Highway 1806 bridge. Here you will enter a small badlands area with several severely eroded buttes. Watch here for turkey vultures, Swainson's and ferruginous hawks." Such information is excellent, particularly when you are searching for "specialties," raptor species that are either rare or locally uncommon.

The ABA/Lane Guides cover some of North America's best birding areas but are not available for every place in the country. Most states and provinces, however, have some form of bird-finding guide that will highlight good raptor areas. State guides usually cover the state in detail and can be an excellent tool for finding raptors near your hometown. For instance, *Where to Find Birds in New York State*, by Susan Drennan, not only has information on all regions of the state, but also has a chapter devoted exclusively to hawkwatching. In it, urban opportunities for hawk-watching such as Robert Moses State Park on Fire Island are detailed, along with how-to information for such classic spots as Mount Peter, Derby Hill and Braddock Bay. *A Bird Finding Guide to Canada*, edited by J.C. Finlay, offers similar information on all the Canadian provinces, with raptors getting good coverage throughout.

To learn if a birding guide is available for your state or area, consult the American Birding Association's *ABA Sales Annotated Catalog and Price List* for a complete inventory of regional guides, arranged by state for the U. S., by province for Canada and by country for the rest of the world (see page 132 for address). Nature centers usually have a bookstore that showcases local bird-finding guides. For some areas, birding information is available on the county or even the municipal level. Several New Jersey counties and most California counties have comprehensive county guides, and due to their popularity, hawks and eagles are usually featured.

While at your local nature center, inquire about their field trips. Nature centers and bird observatories often offer hawk-oriented bird walks or "hawk walks," and hawk-identification workshops, particularly during the migration season. If any established hawkwatches are nearby, there will probably be scheduled vigils. Participating in one or more of these will give you the invaluable chance to learn from the experts. They will know the geography of the area, when and where to look, and what conditions are the most conducive to hawk migration. From there you can branch out on your own. For winter hawk finding,

consider participating in your local Christmas Bird Count. More than 1,500 National Audubon Society Christmas Bird Counts are

Two of hawkwatching and hawk conservation's "greats" discussing the fine points of raptor identification: the late Harold Axtell, *left*, and Hawk Mountain's Jim Brett, *right*.

held across North America. Learn whom to contact from a local bird club or nature center, or write to National Audubon Society *Field Notes* at 700 Broadway, NY, NY 10003 (212-979-3000). Most count groups, or "parties," certainly do not mind additional spotters. Even if you are not an expert birder, tag along and learn—everyone begins as a novice. By participating in an annual winter census, you'll be introduced to the local hotspots. Then you can return on your own to explore throughout the seasons. By birding with groups of experienced watchers, you can bypass or speed up many of the difficult early stages of your raptor education.

Through the Seasons

THE COHANSEY RIVER was choked with ice. A February deep freeze ten days before had brought true winter to the Delaware Bayshore. Snow geese had gathered in enormous numbers on the vast farm fields along the lower river, blending in with the rare winter snowfall, giving the impression of a moving mass of white. Some were still arriving, pushed by cold weather to the north; others were leaving, heading for warmer climes, perhaps the lower Chesapeake. Because we had been conducting weekly surveys as part of a conservation project, we knew that the several immature bald eagles coursing the river were new arrivals, refugees from the frozen North, augmenting the small local population. Between eagles, vultures and clamoring geese, there was a kaleidoscope of sound and movement over the river marshes.

Today, however, a hint of spring was in the air. The late February sun had gained in angle and strength, and the ice on the tidal river was beginning to break up. The thermometer barely broke 40 degrees F, but after the previous ten days, the sun felt good.

The raptors responded. They were slow in getting up, but then began to circle—a kettle of vultures here, a pair of red-tails there. Both a kestrel and a rough-leg hovered where marsh met farmland. On the salt hay meadows near the mouth of the river, a male harrier spotted a prospective partner or his returning mate. He struggled for altitude over her, and began the looping, cartwheeling flight for which

In winter, scan river edges for bald eagles and buteos, *above*. Bald eagles, *right*, are one of the earliest nesting raptors.

harriers are so well known—aptly named sky dancing. As the harriers drifted to the west toward Bayside, we spotted the local bald eagles refurbishing their four-year-old nest in preparation for the coming breeding season.

Soon after, we watched a male red-tail in his courtship flight—an undulating, zooming, diving, roller-coaster display—as he courted a female circling below. He broke off and pumped for altitude. We soon saw why. Another red-tail, high in the sun, was flapping and gliding in off Delaware Bay—a spring migrant. We heard the local male calling as he circled with the intruder, then escorted him through his territory. The new red-tail disappeared due north, perhaps to a New York State woodlot, perhaps to an Ontario river valley. The local male glided down, perching within a few inches of his mate in a red maple. Somehow all seemed right with the world.

There are no hard-and-fast rules about what constitutes fall, winter or spring in the raptor world. That February day, we had spotted immature bald eagles, late migrants fleeing from the frozen North. We also had seen local harriers and local red-tails deep into their spring courtship. Finally, we had watched bald eagles nest building. As one of the earliest breeding raptors (along with great horned owls), bald eagles sometimes lay eggs as early as mid-February along the shores of the Delaware Estuary. So in the same day, in the same place, we had wintering raptors, spring migration, courtship and nesting activity. Although the expected delineations of the seasons are distorted when it comes to raptor behavior, each season still calls for a different approach to spotting hawks and eagles.

Breeding Season

DEPENDING ON WHERE YOU LIVE in North America, the breeding season can be the easiest time to spot raptors—or the hardest. In the far North, where snow cover is heavy, many or most raptors are absent in winter, returning north in spring to begin the breeding cycle anew. Here, raptors will be much more diverse and numerous in the breeding season than in winter. In the lower part of the continent, however, the breeding season can be one of the most difficult times to find raptors. The wintering species are gone, and breeding species become secretive to protect their nest sites, eggs or young. This is also the time when forest-dwelling species (like accipiters, red-shoulders and broad-wings) stay almost entirely within the woods and are not readily spotted.

Most of the breeding season secrecy is limited to the period between egg laying and fledging of the young. Outside of this time span, there are bonuses for the raptor watcher. During courtship, hawks and eagles can be highly visible. Mated pairs of red-tails and bald eagles sit side by side, making them easier to spot. Males perform conspicuous courtship flights high over marsh, field or forest. Also, nest building is obvious: ospreys, red-tails and eagles can often be watched constructing or renovating their nests. Look for green sprigs woven into a nest—a sure sign that a raptor is using it. During breeding season, hawks are highly vocal, and it is usually the only time of the year when you will hear falcons and accipiters calling. To learn raptor calls, listen to commercially available CDs or

Secretive breeding species, such as red-shoulders, will often reveal themselves by call.

tapes of bird songs (see Further Information, page 132). Play the calls at home so you will recognize them in the field. Often secretive breeding species, such as broad-wings, red-shoulders or Cooper's hawks, will reveal themselves by call.

While some use the playback of taped raptor calls to elicit a response from breeding raptors as a means of locating them, we strongly advise against this. Hawks are very sensitive to disturbance during the breeding season, and the provocation of a territorial response or nest defense in response to a presumed intruder (the taped recording) could become a factor in nest failure. Only use taped calls when participating in a bona fide official survey, and

then use them sparingly. They are not really necessary. Careful observation and listening during the nesting season should be all that is needed to find raptors. Also, there is another danger in playing tapes. The response you get may be more than you bargained for. We have been stooped on (swooped down upon) by red-tails and even a broad-wing when too near their nests (both chance encounters, not while playing tapes). Goshawk attacks are legendary. Playing a tape or approaching too close to a nest usually elicits a fierce territorial nest defense/response. Biologists and bird banders wear helmets and goggles when near a goshawk nest for good reason. Be forewarned: approach a goshawk nest and you could walk away bloody. Peregrines carry out a similarly aggressive nest defense, but you are less likely to encounter a peregrine aerie on a cliff face than you are a goshawk nest in the forest.

The Sanctity of Nests

FINDING RAPTOR NESTS in the northern forests can be a difficult experience unless one uses clues such as courtship flight, calls, the food begging calls of the young or feeding flights (carrying prey to the young on the nest) by adults. Better to look for nests in the non-breeding season—the late fall and winter—when they are more easily spotted because deciduous trees have lost their leaves. Both *A Field Guide to Birds' Nests* (Peterson Field Guide Series), by Hal Harrison, and *The Birder's Handbook*, by Erlich, Dobkin and Wheye, are full of helpful information about each raptor's nest: habitat, height above ground, nest size, structure and hints (for example, that old nests are sometimes repaired in autumn and that green sprigs are constantly renewed during incubation). Some species, such as ospreys and eagles, almost always reuse their nest sites; others, such as red-tails, sometimes do. Many, including all accipiters, make new nests each year. They will, however, often nest near their old site. We know of one pair of goshawks that has nested within the same square mile for at least five years. Because of raptors' sensitivity to disturbance, we do not recommend searching for nests in the breeding season. The birds are easily disturbed, and you do not want to be the cause for nest failure—allowing a crow or some other predator to get the eggs while the adults are distracted by you, or providing a scent trail for a raccoon to locate the nest.

If you do find an active raptor nest, enjoy it from a distance. Only visit once every two weeks at most. Nests of those species listed as endangered or threatened in your state or province should never be approached. Never go near a bald eagle nest, not even in fall or winter, because resident eagles often use them as perches or roost sites throughout the year. Although watching raptor nests can be a thrill, you must watch from a distance that will not disturb the occupants. If you can't see it from a distance, so be it. You will eventually find another. When we discovered our first eagle's nest, we watched it from over a mile away with a scope, and even then not often. Eventually, in Florida, we found a "roadside" eagle's nest just sev-

Black hawks and zone-tailed hawks nest in the cottonwoods along Aravaipa Creek, Arizona.

How to Spot Hawks & Eagles

eral hundred yards away, and watched juveniles testing their wings. We took the precaution to stay in our car—using it as a blind.

Always keep nesting raptors' welfare foremost in your mind. Never tell anyone of a nest site you have found. The news may spread to overzealous photographers, illicit falconers, even illegal egg collectors. We know of one case where a birder excitedly told a local farmer about the red-tailed hawk nest and young he had just found. He returned a week later to the remote location to find the young dead in the nest. The pattern of shotgun pellets in the beech tree's bark told the story all too well.

In the West, look for "whitewash" (dried whitish excrement) on exposed bluffs and cliff faces to give away a prairie falcon's nesting location.

Lure of the West

IN THE EAST in summer, you usually have to work for your hawks, hiking forest trails and looking for clues. Your efforts are often met with little success and are accompanied by mosquitoes and ticks. But in the prairie grassland and desert regions of the West, finding a raptor nest can be as easy as finding a tree. Nest sites are at a premium, and lone trees, often near water pumps or tanks, are avidly chosen. Windmills, transmission-line towers and telephone poles in remote regions are sometimes selected as well. You can cruise back roads by car (or bicycle) scanning any elevated perches that may have raptors or nests. In the Southwest, saguaro cactus are commonly used as nest sites by red-tails and Harris' hawks. Stream corridors are also productive. Any sizable creek is usually lined with cottonwoods, and these will be used for perching, roosting and nest building.

Scan bluffs and cliff faces for golden eagle and falcon aeries in the West. Prairie and peregrine falcons nest on exposed bluffs and buttes. Look for "whitewash" or dried whitish excrement to give away a falcon's nesting location. Golden eagles nest in similar situations on steep, inaccessible cliffs. We have found eagle aeries in Ramsey Canyon in Arizona and in Joshua Tree National Monument in California by scanning cliffs over which eagles were seen soaring, and finding whitewash stains below ledges on the cliff faces. Remember that ravens also nest in similar locations and produce copious whitewash. Never approach an eagle or falcon aerie once located, either from above or below. Enjoy it from a distance with your telescope.

One of the finest raptor-watching opportunities anywhere in North America is available in the West during the breeding season. Snake River Birds of Prey Natural Area, near Boise, Idaho, hosts the largest gathering of nesting raptors in the lower 48 states. The natural area consists of about 500,000 acres of rugged river canyons and cliffs along an 80 mile stretch of the Snake River in southwestern Idaho. Much of the surrounding area is managed for raptors as well. The Snake River area is famous for its large numbers of nesting golden eagles, ferruginous hawks, Swainson's hawks and prairie falcons. Various roads and trails run through the area, and there are impressive overlooks. The hawkwatching opportunities are good at all seasons, but particularly in spring and summer.

Large numbers of ferruginous hawks nest along the cliffs of the Snake River in Idaho.

The Snake River is one of the most accessible of the western cliff-nesting areas. Other spectacular aggregations of nesting raptors can be seen in northern Alaska. The Colville River on the north slope of the Brooks Range flows to the Arctic Ocean near Prudhoe Bay. Here, cliffs rise from the tundra and provide homes for rough-legged hawks, golden eagles, peregrines and gyrfalcons during the short Arctic summer. The Meade River and Noatak River provide similar habitat and nesting opportunities. Accessible only by float plane or float trip, we are told that these rivers provide some of the best wilderness birding and raptor watching available on the continent. Denali National Park, north of Anchorage, is far more accessible and can provide many raptor opportunities. Golden and bald eagles are easily seen in summer, and many birders we know have spotted gyrfalcons there.

Winter Season

"THIS IS THE MOST BEAUTIFUL RAPTOR I've ever seen," said David Sibley quietly, without taking his binoculars from his eyes. Over us, an adult dark-form ferruginous hawk circled, hanging on the winter wind briefly before it turned on the downwind leg of its arc. The low afternoon winter sun illuminated the bird. The rusty color on the upper parts continued onto the flanks and belly of the dark hawk. The head was grayish, and silvery flight feathers completed the tricolor pattern. As the bird gained altitude, it was joined by a second, light-form ferruginous hawk and finally by a third. They moved across the alfalfa field and finally became specks against the foothills

The rusty back against the light underparts make the ferruginous hawk a spotter's delight.

of the Chiricahuas to the east. David lowered his binoculars and began drawing rapidly, the image of the "ferrug" appearing on his sketch pad. As we walked back to the van, a prairie falcon on a late hunting mission dashed behind the nearby hay bales and crossed the lowering sun. Southeast Arizona offers world-class birding at any time of the year, but the Sulphur Springs Valley, between Willcox to the north and Douglas on the Mexican border, is a mecca for winter birding and for raptor enthusiasts in particular. Highway 191 runs through the heart of the valley, a landlocked basin that drains into a large, usually dry, alkaline lake known as the Willcox Playa. This former grassland is now mostly farmland, but hay is a principal crop and birds abound. Elfrida, Arizona, is the epicenter of the valley. We first learned of it by paging through the annual Christmas Bird Count results published in National Audubon Society's *American Birds*. Elfrida kept popping up in the list of national high counts for many species. The numbers of ferruginous hawks and prairie falcons reported were among the highest in the nation, and the raptor diversity was excellent. So when planning a trip to study western raptors, the Sulphur Springs Valley is a must. Virtually all of it is private property, but the birding along seldom-traveled back roads can

Two prime winter raptor sites: Sulphur Springs Valley, Arizona *top,* and Blackwater NWR on the Chesapeake Bay, *bottom.*

be extraordinary. Contact the Southeastern Arizona Bird Observatory for winter raptor offerings (see page 134.)

In many areas of the continent, winter is the easiest time to spot raptors. Because so many birds, both prey species and birds of prey, migrate south to warmer climates, winter finds them concentrated geographically south of deep snow cover. A few hawks and eagles stay north in winter throughout Canada and the northern U.S., but snow-free coastal areas and the southern tier of the United States hold far more.

The Sulphur Springs Valley is just one of many prime areas. Oklahoma is a winter raptor capital, and hundreds of red-tails can be seen along roadsides there in winter, even along the Interstates. Texas is another definitive destination for winter hawks and eagles. In the northern Texas panhandle, visit places like Muleshoe NWR and Buffalo Lake NWR. Bosque del Apache NWR in New Mexico is well known for waterfowl and cranes in winter, but this 58,000-acre refuge hosts numerous hawks and eagles too.

Because of moderate temperatures and ice-free waters, coastlines are particularly good places to find wintering raptors. On the East Coast, Parker River NWR and the nearby Merrimack River in Massachusetts hold bald eagles and rough-legged hawks (and snowy owls) every winter, and gyrfalcons have been spotted there a number of times. Farther south, the Delaware Bayshore in both New Jersey and Delaware is well known for wintering raptors, particularly New Jersey's Maurice and Cohansey Rivers. The Chesapeake region has vast open space, and hawks and eagles are commonplace. The Chesapeake Bay has the largest winter bald eagle concentration in the East, north of Florida. Our favorite spot is Blackwater NWR in Dorchester County, Maryland. It is a highly scenic tidal wetlands

How to Spot Hawks & Eagles

refuge, packed with waterfowl in winter. It is not uncommon to see 40 to 50 bald eagles a day in the Blackwater area (we have seen 20 at once here), and usually a golden eagle or two are present. Red-tails, harriers and black and turkey vultures abound.

Almost all natural areas in Florida are excellent raptor locations. Many bald eagles reside here, augmented in winter by legions of birds from the north. Try the Lake Region for winter eagles. One of our favorite destinations is Lake Kissimmee State Park, near Lake Wales, where 10 to 20 eagles can be seen on a winter day (many are present all year). Caracaras are also found here, and in spring you should be able to spot swallow-tailed kites. The entire Florida prairie region, north and west of Lake Okeechobee, is good for hawk viewing in winter. Red-tails, American kestrels, bald eagles and ospreys are present in generous numbers. There is usually a western rarity or two found each winter, such as Krider's red-tailed hawk or ferruginous hawk, and the Florida prairies are the only place in the east where crested caracaras are found. In addition, this area (including the Everglades) is the only region of the country where snail kites can be seen. They move around from season to season and from year to year in response to changing water levels and the related availability of their food: apple snails. Call birding hotlines for up-to-date information on snail kites and their whereabouts.

The Florida Everglades, and particularly Everglades National Park, is another great location for watching raptors in winter. Bald eagles, ospreys, vultures and red-shouldered hawks are abundant and easily spotted. Also, this is the easiest time and place to find short-tailed hawks; up to ten have been seen on the Flamingo Christmas Bird Count. They concentrate in the southern Everglades, migrating there from northern and central Florida.

The Gulf Coast is excellent in winter as well. At 145,000 acres, Sabine NWR in southwestern Louisiana near Lake Charles offers a wide variety of birds, including raptors. Peregrine and merlin are usually present. The lower Texas coast is a raptor mecca in winter. Wintering red-tails are abundant (and available in all plumages) and resident Harris' hawks, white-tailed hawks and white-tailed kites are found. Try Routes 77 and 281 between Corpus Christi and Harlingen. For best results, spend time around Kingsville and at Laguna Atascosa NWR. Consult the ABA/Lane Birdfinding Guides (see page 131) for specific raptor directions.

The West Coast has some prime raptor spots too. The agricultural and grassland valleys of California are good: Central Valley, Carrizo Plain, Cuyama Valley, Antelope Valley and Owen's Valley. In the Northwest, the Klamath Basin has great numbers and diversity of raptors. The Skagit Flats area, north of Seattle, is possibly the most dependable place in the lower 48 states to see gyrfalcons; two or three are present most winters. Some lucky observers have seen gyrfalcons, peregrines, prairie falcons, merlins and American kestrels in the same day, and we've read of one person who had all of them in view at once. The Dungeness area on the Strait of Juan de Fuca usually has a gyrfalcon or two in winter. Try Dungeness NWR, San Juan NWR, and Jones Island NWR. Gyrfalcons are also seen every winter in the Fraser Delta area, west of Ladner, British Columbia, or along the nearby shores of Boundary Bay. Gyrs are enough of a rarity anywhere in the lower 48 that if one is located, it will be reported on birding hotlines. These are usually updated weekly or even daily when "good birds" are around. To find hotline numbers for where you live or where you are traveling, consult bird-finding guides for the region or ask at parks or nature centers. The American Birding Association prints a list regularly in their publication, *Winging It*. The locations of eagle concentrations are also usually reported on hotlines.

Bald Eagle Bonanzas

TO FIND BALD EAGLES in winter, focus on coasts, rivers, watercourses and reservoirs. Eagles leave the frozen North and concentrate in spectacular numbers in several places. The National Wildlife Refuges of the Klamath Basin on the California-Oregon border are among the most exciting in North America, with concentrations of waterfowl reaching several million in late fall. As many as 1,000 bald eagles winter here, the largest number outside of Alaska, and sometimes several hundred can be seen from the same vantage point. Both the Lower Klamath unit and the Tule Lake units there are a must for the birder, photographer or eagle spotter.

Another significant winter aggregation of eagles is found at Squaw Creek NWR in Missouri, where as many as 250 bald eagles and a few golden eagles can be found in late fall and early winter. Be sure to visit before the Missouri River freezes. Final freeze-up, usually in early January, pushes the waterfowl south, and many eagles leave to follow them. Call ahead for details. Reelfoot Lake in Tennessee is also a good eagle spot. Other winter eagle concentrations can be found at Glacier National Park (over 300 in a day) between October and mid-December, where they feed on salmon; at Olympic National Park on the Olympic Peninsula in Washington; and at the North Cascades National Park Complex along the Skagit River, also in Washington.

The largest gathering of bald eagles in the world occurs October through December each year on the Chilkat River near Haines, Alaska (north of Juneau). Up to 4,000 in one day have been seen here, drawn by salmon runs. This phenomenon is quite accessible. Head north out of Haines on Haines Highway (State Route 7) to mile

No raptor watcher's list is complete without at least one sighting of the majestic bald eagle.

How to Spot Hawks & Eagles

Each year, the largest gathering of bald eagles in the world occurs along the Chilkat River near Haines, Alaska, where up to 4,000 have been counted in one day.

marker 19, where large numbers of birds can be seen from the roadside. Scan the forest edge, river shoreline and river. Do not leave the roadside—it will disturb the eagles.

In the East, find bald eagles in winter along rivers and reservoirs. The Delaware River from Port Jervis, New York, to the Delaware Water Gap north of Stroudsburg, Pennsylvania, usually holds 30 to 40 eagles in winter, and the Hudson River has many dependable eagle-observation points. Open water below dams and reservoirs attracts these raptors, usually drawn to the fish found there. The Conowingo Dam in northeastern Maryland and the Susquehanna River in Pennsylvania are prime eagle areas in winter. Quabbin Reservoir in Massachusetts hosts up to 50 bald eagles and usually a golden eagle or two. Eagles are often seen sitting on the ice of the frozen lake. Try the Enfield lookout off Route 9 for a start. Consult the ABA's *Birder's Guide to Eastern Massachusetts* for in-depth access information.

In areas where eagles congregate in winter, parks or nature centers often hold "eagle outings" or festivals where organized eagle-viewing field trips are offered for the public. (See pages 132-135 for a list of organized events.)

Migration

THE COLD FRONT swept across the Jersey coast pre-dawn on September 23, 1981 and as the skies began clearing, sharp-shins were already on the wing at first light, coming down the treeline and washing over the hawkwatch like waves on a sandbar. Even on the first day, we realized something was different. No one could remember such a strong front so early in the season. The jet stream had dipped south, and the front had roared across the continent in just three days, bringing snow to the Rockies and northern Great Plains. At Cape May, the early morning sky was raptor-ridden and awash with tree swallows, bobolinks, warblers and flocks of hundreds of cormorants. As the morning progressed, the steady stream of sharp-shins low over the trees slowly gave way to American kestrels passing by in loose groups, fighting the northwest gale. Merlins punctuated the flight, racing dark and low over the pond and out beyond Saint Mary's and the Cape May Point Lighthouse. At final tally, well over 1,000 sharp-shins and 3,500 kestrels had been counted that day.

The second morning dawned, with clear skies. The winds held northwest and strong, sweeping migratory raptors to the coast, where they then concentrated at Cape May Point. Hawks, neither inclined nor designed to fly over water, faced the 13-mile-wide Delaware Bay. With the winds so strong, and the danger of being blown to sea, raptors began to fill up the Cape May peninsula like water filling a jug. Over 75 percent of coastal mi-

Blustery cold fronts trigger raptor flights in fall. *Above*, a cold front clears Cape May at dusk. *Right*, an osprey on the wing heads south.

How to Spot Hawks & Eagles

During migration, northern harriers do not hesitate to cross water barriers.

grant raptors are that year's young, a much higher percentage than is found at inland ridges. In many cases, the immatures have been out of the nest less than a month. For these young hawks, the Delaware Bay is the first major body of water they have ever seen.

The second day, Cooper's hawks joined the sharp-shins, and turkey vultures low over the trees were buffeted by the wind. A steady stream of harriers and ospreys headed unhesitatingly out over the "bunker" to the Delaware Bay and south. These two species show no fear of crossing water. In the afternoon, several peregrines appeared. Finally, a bald eagle showed up—first high over Cape May City, and then lumbering down the treeline past the

watch, thrilling all. This was well before bald eagles (and peregrines) had recovered from the ravages of DDT, and each bald eagle sighting was an event cherished by watchers. Again, the sunset tally showed over 1,000 sharp-shins, 2,000 kestrels, 113 ospreys and 97 harriers—another great day and one with the promise of more to come.

The most unusual feature of these first two days was the broad-winged hawks' movement against the wind. They fought their way over the coastal marsh and over Cape May City, to gain the shelter of the trees at Cape May Point State Park and at Higbee Beach WMA. This massive cold front had coincided with the peak time for their migration, and many had been

How to Spot Hawks & Eagles

pushed to the brink, to the beaches of the Atlantic Ocean. For two days, we watched them pumping in, away from the ocean, filling up the Cape. That evening, we spoke excitedly with other veteran watchers about the next day's prospects, which seemed auspicious.

The following morning was clear and still. Soon after dawn, a gentle north wind began to blow, and brush strokes of high cirrus painted the sky. An hour after sunrise, sharp-shins again filled the sky, and on the kinder winds, Cooper's hawks began soaring in small groups. On the treeline, out over Pond Creek Marsh, small kettles of broad-wings began to form, and then grow, birds multiplying in the sky almost exponentially, as swarms began to convene. As the sun rose higher and better thermals developed, pure magic occurred. Almost as if on cue, the broad-wings all came out of the soaring kettles and began streaming, gliding toward the hawkwatch. Soon there was a solid sheet of hawks stretching from Cape May City to Cape May Point, and then north up the Delaware Bayshore to Higbee Beach, a sheet of hawks four miles long and a half-mile wide. With hurried rough calculations, we guessed that 7,000 broad-wings were overhead.

As they slowly lost altitude, kettles began reforming—boiling masses of circling hawks all over the sky. Inevitably, the birds began dispersing, getting higher and farther out and disappearing to the north. These hawks would not cross the Delaware Bay here, but would fly north and west around it to continue their annual autumnal journey to South America. As the sky cleared of hawks, we began to reflect on what we had seen. Cape May only sees large numbers of broad-wings every eight or ten years—normally they take inland routes, over Hawk Mountain in Pennsylvania, for example. But in over 20 years of hawkwatching at Cape May, September 25, 1981 remains one of the most memorable days for us— hawkwatching at its finest.

The migration of birds has always intrigued and excited humans. As Rich Stallcup, an ardent observer of nature, wrote (in the Point Reyes Bird Observatory newsletter): "Migration holds observable magic and proof that Earth has a pulse. Most migration takes place at night and is only detectable by the appearance of many birds one morning where there were none the day before, or perhaps by small voices heard in a dark sky. To be able to *see* and *feel* this great and mystical phenomenon is a very special experience. Because many large birds move during the day, Earth's poetry is strongly laced with visions of them."

Hawks and eagles, perhaps more so than any other birds save geese, are highly visible migrants, and as such allow us to feel and experience the heartbeat of migration.

While not every outing is as dramatic as the red-letter days at Cape May described above, hawk migration can be readily witnessed. At many established hawkwatching sites throughout the continent, you can see more hawks in one day during migration than you might see in a year's casual birding. And if you hit the timing of the migration and the weather just right, you might see more hawks in a day than in a lifetime. The migration seasons are, by far, your best opportunity to spot numbers of hawks and eagles because of their temporal (seasonal) and spatial (geographic) concentrations.

Geography

BECAUSE BIRDS ARE LEAVING their natal home and established, known territories, venturing out over unfamiliar lands and habitats, migration is the toughest time in their life cycle. Often far from their breeding ranges and preferred habitats, they become vulnerable to predators and to lack of food, habitat and stopover sites. At migration "bottlenecks" they can often be seen in enormous numbers.

To spot hawks and eagles during migration, simply place yourself in opportunity's way. Raptors migrate on a broad front, but their movements are directed and numbers concentrated by "leading lines." Think of leading lines as raptor roadways, which direct hawks south in the fall and north in the spring. These lines include mountain ridges like the ones at Hawk Mountain in Pennsylvania, Mount Tom in Massachusetts or Hook Mountain in New York, where raptors are drawn to energy-conserving updrafts. Hawk Mountain is such an important site because the Kittatinny Ridge is the last ridge—with the last updrafts—before birds head out over flatlands that stretch all the way to the coast.

Leading lines also include the shorelines of lakes and coasts, producing terrific concentrations like those at Cape May, New Jersey, and Duluth, Minnesota, in fall, and at Braddock Bay, New York, and Whitefish Point, Michigan, in spring. Remember that raptors travel either by using updrafts off mountain ridges (deflected winds) or by using thermals (rising columns of warm air) to gain easy lift. Because thermals do not form over water, hawks elect to stay along shorelines, avoiding oceans and large lakes. With prevailing northwest winds carrying birds to the east, the Atlantic coastline acts as a giant leading line in fall, particularly for falcons and accipiters. As birds hit the coast and turn south, sites such as Cape May and Kiptopeke (Cape Charles) in Virginia concentrate the raptors from thousands of square miles of northern forest onto a ten-square-mile tip of the peninsulas. It is this phenomenon of concentration that made the hawk shooting of the 1920s and 1930s so insidious at Cape May and at Hawk Mountain. It is also why the habitat at such migration crossroads is of critical national importance and must be protected.

Weather

WEATHER CONDITIONS play a major role in hawk migration, affecting when and what numbers might be seen at a certain location. During the fall, cold fronts trigger the migratory urge in birds, and the generally north or northwest winds associated with a high pressure area behind a cold front propel birds south. As Pete Dunne explained in his column in *Wild Bird* (July 1995), "For some thermal-dependent species, such as broad-winged hawks, these cold fronts not only force them south, they actually carry them. Northwest winds associated with a passing front sweep migrating birds with them in the same way that a person swimming across a river is propelled downstream."

Raptors are flying south, on a broad front, but are also being carried east, into leading lines such as mountain ridges and shorelines. In addition, some species seem to travel ahead

Mountain ridges, coastlines and shorelines serve as "leading lines" for raptor migration in both spring and fall, offering excellent hawkwatching opportunities. *Top:* Hawk Mountain, Pennsylvania; *bottom*, Grand Mere Dunes State Park on Lake Michigan.

pre-frontal. Their best flights generally come on easterly winds the day before a cold front passes.

Warm fronts trigger spring migration at most locations. As early as late February, even at northerly locations like Braddock Bay on the south shore of Lake Ontario, raptors push north, propelled by warm, southerly breezes. Each spring, adult raptors head north as soon as their breeding grounds are habitable in an effort to be the first to claim the choicest nest sites. This explains why red-tails are such early spring migrants—because they are heading to New York, Ohio and Missouri, and why peregrines are late-season migrants—heading for the Arctic tundra, which does not defrost until June.

If you plan to visit a migration juncture, first decide which species you wish to see and when their peak migration period occurs. If you want to see spring red-tailed hawks at Braddock Bay, somewhere around March 21 to March 31 is usually when the peak movement occurs, and around April 25 is best for broad-winged hawks. In fall, at Hawk Mountain for example, September 17 is the magic date for broad-wings, and the best flights of golden eagles usually occur the first week of November. Once you have

of cold fronts, as if they were skirting them to stay ahead of the colder weather. At Cape May, ospreys and peregrines are notoriously inquired about timing, try, if at all possible, to plan your trip to coincide with a front. In fall, cold fronts produce the best flights, from

Duluth to Point Pelee and Holiday Beach, to Hawk Mountain and Cape May. Watch "The Weather Channel," or listen to NOAA weather radio broadcasts to learn when cold fronts will sweep across the continent. Television weather maps usually show fronts well. At ridge locations such as Hawk Mountain, the first day of the front is usually the best, when strong winds create good updrafts and give raptors a "free ride." At coastal locations like Cape May, which depend on raptors being "carried" in, the second day after the front passes is often best, providing the wind holds from the northwest. These are broad generalizations, and local conditions such as sun and cloud cover can be critical. Broad-wings in particular move en masse and are the most thermal-dependent raptors. For these reasons, they are often missed at key locations despite wind, weather and timing all seeming perfect. There are many stories of hawkwatchers waiting in vain at a lookout while, ten miles away, someone watching from the roadside sees 20,000 broad-wings in an hour.

In spring, warm fronts spur migration and are the key to good flights at such spots as Whitefish Point in Michigan and Braddock Bay in New York. In our own experience, spring warm fronts are harder to predict than fall cold fronts, and a lot of meteorological pieces need to fall into place for a surging spring warm front to sweep north. Nonetheless, when they do they often last several days, and raptors pulse north. Once again, local conditions can play an important role. Many are the tales of woe from lakefront sites of strong warm fronts negated by "lake effect" winds (off the lake), pushing hawks well in-land away from shoreline leading lines and waiting watchers.

Fall Migration Hotspots

GEOGRAPHY and prevailing weather combine to create a number of places in North America that stand out as true migration hotspots. Here, on a regular basis, binocular meets raptor—lots of raptors. The flights at many of these places can be legendary and can give you more raptor experience in a few days than you might gain in years of breeding season or winter watching. As a raptor aficionado, you should try to visit most of these hotspots at least once.

Hawk Mountain, Pennsylvania, is where it all began. It was here in 1934 that Maurice Broun and Rosalie Edge confronted the slaughter of migrating hawks by "sportsmen," and in the process founded Hawk Mountain Sanctuary and began organized migration counts and hawkwatching. Pete Dunne has called it the "godfather site" of hawkwatching, a seminal place to which we owe so much. A trip to Hawk Mountain takes you back to the roots of spotting, counting and enjoying hawks and eagles. Near Reading, Pennsylvania, the mountain is a ridge site, offering a panoramic view of the Kittatinny Mountains, and on the right winds, affording point-blank views of hawks and eagles. If you go in peak season, mid-September to mid-October, expect crowds. Hawk Mountain is immensely popular. Our favorite time is red-tail season, in mid-November, when if you go on a weekday, there will be just a few hardy stalwarts on the lookout. Plan to go after a cold front passes and the winds are from the northwest.

About 25,000-30,000 raptors are counted at Hawk Mountain each autumn. These counts, carried on since 1934, have alerted biologists to the precipitous drop in raptor populations in the 1960s due to the use of DDT and have charted their recovery since its ban. Similar hawk counts are conducted at virtually all hawk migration sites. Such grass-roots research documents long-term status and trends of raptor species, irruptive migrations, and the effects of weather on migration.

At most key migration sites, there is an official counter whose job it is to identify and log passing birds as carefully as possible. As the birds fly by, they are clicked off one by one on hand-held numerical counters. At ridge sites, this can be fairly straightforward, but at coastal peninsulas, counting can be a real challenge as the birds mill about at the water barrier. Then it takes a counter's patience and thorough familiarity with the flight and its path in order to eliminate double counting. A broad front movement or big flight taxes even the most experienced counter. Cape May Bird Observatory has conducted a number of studies to test the accuracy of its counts (using visible tail tags on banded raptors, radio telemetry and additional counts at nearby sites). The results have upheld the surprising reliability of counts obtained by the official hawk counter.

At many sites, hawk banding is conducted in conjunction with hawk counting. Experienced banders trap and tag raptors with U.S. Fish and Wildlife Service bands. This practice provides significant information about raptor

Many hawkwatch sites provide raptor banding demonstrations for the public. Here, Chris Schultz displays a northern harrier at Cape May Point State Park in New Jersey.

populations and migration. At Braddock Bay, Cape May, Golden Gate, Duluth and several of HawkWatch International's western sites (Goshutes, Manzanos and Sandias), banding demonstrations are conducted frequently during peak season (see pages 132-135). At these programs, given by a naturalist, you can see hawks up close and learn about raptor biology and migration. It is always a thrill to see a raptor released to continue its migration, carrying the newly placed bird band. When any of these bands are recovered, they give biologists invaluable data about the bird's movements and longevity.

In addition to Hawk Mountain, there are numerous excellent fall migration watch sites in the East. Some of the more famous are Mount Wachusett, in Massachusetts near Princeton, where, in a good year, over 20,000 hawks are seen in a season. Also in Massachusetts, Mount Tom, near Holyoke, has good fall flights. Farther south, Hook Mountain, near Nyack, and Mount Peter, near Greenwood Lake in New York State, have excellent and popular fall lookouts. Near New York City, Montclair, New Jersey, is a key watch site, and a hawk count is conducted from early September through November each year. Spring flights are good here too. It is an urban watch site, located on the Watchung Ridge, but offers a wonderful panorama and an excellent window on hawk flights skirting New York City on their way south. Usually about 30,000 hawks a year are counted here—and some years' counts are much higher if the broad-wings cooperate by passing directly over the watch (as opposed to farther inland).

Holiday Beach, 20 miles south of Windsor, Ontario (near Detroit), has proven itself to be one of the best lookouts on the continent. Holiday Beach Conservation Area is the culmination of the leading line along the north shore of Lake Erie. Here, an average of 83,000 raptors are spotted each fall season, as birds following the lakeshore "bottle up" before proceeding south into Michigan and Ohio. Flights are legendary, and one of the largest raptor concentrations in North America occurs here. Across the Detroit River from Holiday Beach, hawks crossing the river concentrate at Lake Erie Metropark in enormous numbers at times. On September 19, 1994, 228,000 broad-winged hawks were counted here, the largest single-day broad-wing flight ever recorded north of southern Texas.

Farther east on Lake Erie, Point Pelee National Park has excellent flights, as does Hawk Cliff, near Port Stanley, Ontario, even farther east. Try Rondeau Provincial Park (between the two) as well.

The same phenomenon of raptor concentration occurs on Lake Superior at Duluth, Minnesota. Duluth remains one of the premier hawkwatching locations anywhere. Here, up to 75,000 birds of prey are recorded each year at Hawk Ridge Nature Reserve, where bluffs rise 800 feet above the Lake Superior shoreline. The view is excellent, and the flights can be spectacular when wind and weather cooperate. More than 5,000 goshawks have been recorded in a good flight year (they are cyclical), and it is particularly known for roughlegs and eagles. Over 700 bald eagles were once counted in a single day. Duluth is a hawkwatching must.

The Atlantic Coast

On the Atlantic Coast, major flights occur each year at Cape May, New Jersey, specifically at the little seaside town of Cape May Point. Here, in the 1930s, Roger Tory Peterson, Witmer Stone and others silenced the guns of hawk hunters. The hawkwatch platform at the Cape May Point State Park affords the best view of the flight. The Cape May Bird Observatory conducts the hawkwatch and records an average of 60,000 raptors each fall. Although 19 species of raptors

Each autumn, migrant peregrines concentrate along Atlantic coastal beaches.

are seen here each year, Cape May is best known for its accipiters and falcons. Over 1,000 peregrines have been seen here in a season, and peak flights of more than 100 in a day occur each year. The first week of October is usually the peak for peregrines, ospreys and accipiters, but cold fronts from mid-September through mid-November can be spectacular, and late season brings greater variety.

An excellent feature of Cape May is the concurrent songbird and seabird migration. Cape May has been called the Raptor Capital of North America—for just cause. Flights may be larger elsewhere, but the dependability and diversity of the flights and the all-around good birding combine to make it a site every hawkwatcher should visit.

Farther down the coast, Cape Charles, Virginia, concentrates hawks in much the same way as Cape May, as hawks are deterred from crossing Chesapeake Bay. A hawkwatch is carried out at Kiptopeke State Park, and numbers are similar to those at Cape May. Falcons and accipiters again predominate, but vulture flocks can be impressive here—the best north of Texas. Assateague and Chincoteague, north of Cape Charles, are known for peregrine flights in fall. Time spent on the beach at Chincoteague NWR will guarantee numerous peregrine sightings during early October.

Hawk flights disperse south of Cape Charles, but Cape Hatteras is a good site for falcons. The next major fall hawk concentrations to the south are in the Florida Keys. No regular watches are established, but part time counts near Marathon have recorded nearly 10,000 raptors in a season. Variety is good, with many falcons, accipiters, vultures and broad-winged hawks. The Keys are the best place in the East to see Swainson's hawks in fall, and short-tailed hawks are seen on migration each year. Choose the south end of any of the Keys, and look northward.

Some raptors cross from the Florida Keys to Cuba and thence to South America, but most use the Gulf Coast as a leading line west, then south. Recently, huge flights have been discovered in Cameron Parish and near Baton Rouge, Louisiana.

The Cape May Bird Observatory conducts a yearly hawk count, recording an average of 60,000 raptors each fall.

The Gulf Coast

THE TEXAS COAST offers some of the best raptor watching in North America, if not the world. Each fall, raptors concentrate in enormous numbers in eastern Texas, and flights of broad-wings and Swainson's hawks are mythical. Over 800,000 raptors have been estimated in a single season passing through south Texas on their way to Mexico. Watches are established at Smith Point, southeast of Houston on the upper coast, and at Hazel Bazemore County Park in Corpus Christi. Here, the Texas Coastal Bend Hawkwatch has recorded over 300,000 raptors in a season. Most are broad-wings, but over 10,000 Mississippi kites and 2,000 Swainson's hawks have been recorded in the fall. The flight can cover a broad front, with part of it inland from the coast. Santa Ana NWR and Bentsen-Rio Grande Valley State Park are excellent autumn concentration sites. Try the dikes on the northern boundaries of these refuges for the best views. Another choice in Texas, South Padre Island, is well known for fall peregrine flights—some of the largest in the nation. Scan the beach, dunes and ocean from any of the dune-crossing overlooks.

South of the border, raptors are geographically concentrated to an even greater extent. In Veracruz, Mexico, where raptors are squeezed tight against the coast by the Sierra Madre Mountains rising dramatically to the west, over 3 million raptors (mostly broad-wings, Swainson's hawks and turkey vultures) have been estimated in a fall season here. On October 11, 1994, Jorge Montejo Diaz counted 925,000 hawks in a single day at Cardel, north of the city of Veracruz. The 1,247,139 raptors counted in two days, that October 11 and 12, make this the world's largest-ever two-day raptor count. Spring flights are mind-boggling as well. Hawkwatching is in its infancy there, but the opportunity to see and count raptors is unbelievable. Panama, the ultimate geographic bottleneck, has similar flights as hawks and vultures enter the South American continent in fall and return north with the spring.

The West

IN WESTERN North America, raptor concentrations are not as great as in the East. Although raptor populations are high in many areas, various western mountain ranges create multiple leading lines. With raptors traveling on many ridges, they are not as concentrated at any one site. Nevertheless, some excellent hawk flights have been discovered. The Goshute Mountains in eastern Nevada host the largest known western raptor flyway. Here, up to 22,000 migrants of 17 species have been recorded in a season by HawkWatch International. Numerous Cooper's hawks, Swainson's hawks, red-tails, ferruginous hawks and golden eagles can be seen.

A hawkwatch in the Bridger Mountains in Montana covers the Front Range of the Rocky Mountains. The site is in Gallatin National Forest, located on the crest of the narrow mountain range above the Bridger Bowl Ski Area near Bozeman. "Only" about 2,500 raptors are seen here each fall season, but over half

of them are golden eagles. More than 1,700 goldens were counted here one year, documenting the Bridgers as one of the major golden eagle routes out of Alaska and the Canadian northwest.

The Wellsville Mountains site near Great Salt Lake in northern Utah records up to

The Grand Canyon is a popular hawkwatching site, combining birding with dramatic scenery.

5,000 hawks each fall, and hawkwatchers in the Manzano Mountains of central New Mexico have seen up to 12,000 in a season, including over 7,000 Swainson's. Lipan Point on the South Rim of the Grand Canyon, Arizona, is becoming a popular site, with over 10,000 birds a season. The view from this site is reportedly exceptional. The Sandia Mountains, east of Albuquerque, New Mexico, are a popular spring watch, with over 5,000 hawks seen some seasons, including a small but regular zone-tailed hawk migration. Generally, hawks are not as well concentrated along western mountain ranges in the spring as they are in the fall.

Another signigficant western event is the coastal flight recorded each fall from the Marin Headlands, on the north side of the Golden Gate Bridge at San Francisco, California. Here, the Golden Gate Raptor Observatory hawkwatch records from 14,000 to 23,000 raptors each season. Variety is great, with 19 species seen most years, including white-tailed kites, red-shoulders, broad-wings (including the rare dark form), ferruginous hawks and prairie falcons. This site combines great access with a memorable view. Contact

The Marin Headlands, on the north side of the Golden Gate Bridge, offer hawkwatching opportunities and a memorable view of San Francisco.

the Golden Gate Raptor Observatory (see page 133). Farther north, the Cape Flattery raptor count at Neah Bay, Washington, records about 5,000 hawks each spring, with red-tails predominating.

Spring Migration Hotspots

THERE ARE NOT NEARLY as many spring watches in North America as fall ones. Warm fronts produce good tail winds and broad front movement, and geography does not tend to create leading lines. But the spring watch sites that do exist are exceptional. In South Texas, Bentsen-Rio Grande Valley State Park and Santa Ana NWR can be spectacular. Part-time hawk counts are done at each spot every spring. Bentsen has recorded up to 78,000 hawks in a season, and Santa Ana sees upwards of 60,000. Over 200,000 have been recorded as a regional total. Turkey vultures, broad-wings and Swainson's hawks predominate. Watch from the dikes on the northern boundaries at both Bentsen and at Santa Ana to witness the river of raptors flowing out of Mexico. The last week of March and the first week of April are best. In addition, kettles of raptors might be encountered almost anywhere along the Texas coast in late March or April; the Kingsville area is particularly good for intercepting northbound hawks.

Few major concentrations occur between Texas and the Great Lakes in spring, but the Great Lakes create many excellent sites. Whitefish Point, in Michigan west of Sault Ste. Marie, concentrates hawks attempting to move east around Lake Superior. Up to 30,000 hawks are seen some years. Counts are conducted and programs given by the Whitefish Point Bird

How to Spot Hawks & Eagles

Observatory. Also in Michigan, the Keeweenaw Peninsula produces significant hawk flights. In southwest Wisconsin, Eagle Valley Nature Center on the Mississippi River is a prime place to spot bald eagles in fall, winter and spring. Recently, 748 were recorded in just 12 days of spring observation.

Farther east, Braddock Bay near Rochester, New York, offers some of the finest hawkwatching in North America. Spring flights here, monitored by Braddock Bay Raptor Research, are becoming legend. Once again, it is the geography that produces high concentrations. At Braddock Bay, the shoreline abruptly turns southwest, and raptors following the southern shore of Lake Ontario become especially concentrated. Over 100,000 raptors have been seen here in a season, although 50,000-60,000 are more the average. Buteos predominate: adult red-tails and red-shoulders early in the season and broad-wings later. Turkey vultures are abundant here also—once 1,900 were seen in a single day. East of Braddock, near Mexico Point, Derby Hill offers another window on hawks skirting the lake. Many are the same birds that pass Braddock, and over 65,000 have been recorded here in spring. At times, the views at Derby are better (closer) than those at Braddock. Both are spots that the avid hawkwatcher simply must visit. One final Great

In the spring, kettles of turkey vultures can readily be spotted gathering over many hawkwatch sites.

Lakes watch is at Grimsby, Ontario. Here, watchers record hawks going around the west end of Lake Ontario, and up to 18,000 raptors have been recorded taking this route north.

A Sampling of Major
Spring and Fall Hawk Migration Sites
~

For a complete list and accounting of the hundreds of hawkwatches conducted across North America, consult the Hawk Migration Association of North America's journal, *Hawk Migration Studies*, where each hawkwatch's seasonal totals are discussed. To obtain this publication, see page 130.

Braddock Bay, New York, at sunset.

SPRING SITES

1. Beamer (Grimsby), Ontario
2. Braddock Bay, New York
3. Derby Hill, New York
4. Sandy Hook, New Jersey
5. Ft. Smallwood, Maryland
6. Whitefish Point, Michigan
7. Sandia Mountains, New Mexico
8. South Texas: Bentsen-Rio Grande State Park
9. South Texas: Santa Ana NWR and vicinity
10. South Padre Island, Texas

FALL SITES

1. Mt. Wachusett, Massachusetts
2. Mt. Peter, New York
3. Lighthouse Point, Connecticut
4. Montclair, New Jersey
5. Hawk Mountain, Pennsylvania
6. Cape May, New Jersey
7. Kiptopeke (Cape Charles), Virginia
8. South Florida (including the Keys)
9. Holiday Beach, Ontario
10. Lake Erie Metropark, Michigan
11. Hawk Ridge (Duluth), Minnesota
12. Bridger Mountains, Montana
13. Wellsville Mountains, Utah
14. Goshute Mountains, Nevada
15. Manzano Mountains, New Mexico
16. Golden Gate (Marin Headlands), California
17. Upper Coast (Smith Point), Texas
18. Coastal Bend (Corpus Christi), Texas

How to Spot Hawks & Eagles

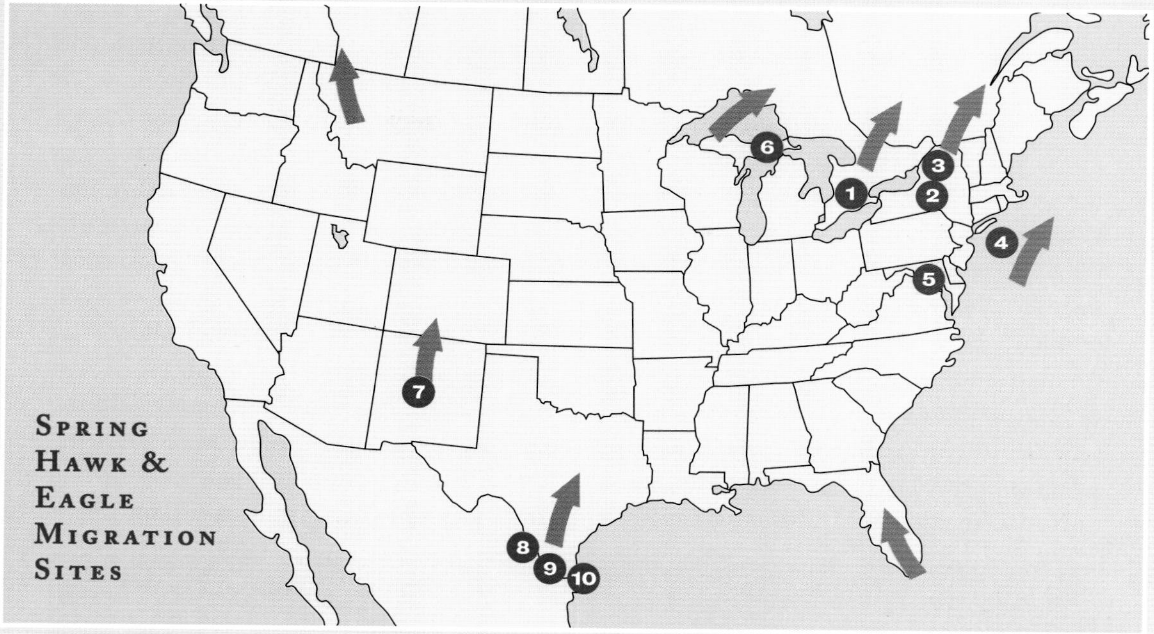
SPRING
HAWK &
EAGLE
MIGRATION
SITES
1
2
3
4
5
6
7
8
9
10

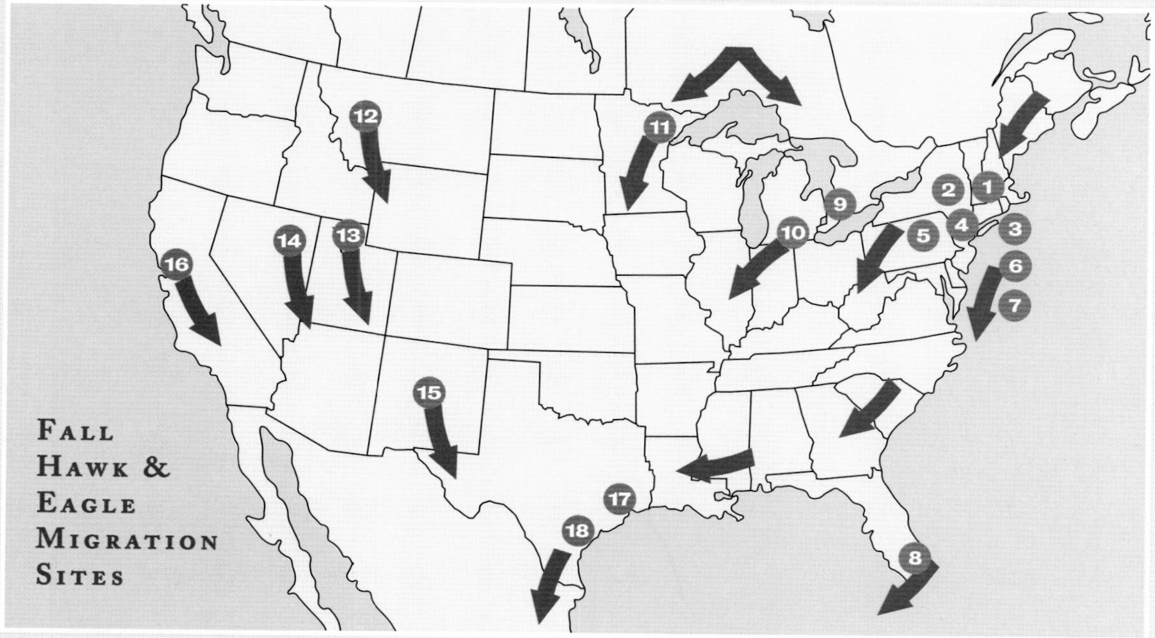
FALL
HAWK &
EAGLE
MIGRATION
SITES
1
2
3
4
5
6
7
8
9
10
11
12
13
14
15
16
17
18

The Hawk Migration Association of North America

WHILE THE ABOVE ACCOUNTS detail the best known hawk observation hotspots, there are hundreds, indeed thousands, of other excellent places on the continent to find raptors. No doubt many are yet to be discovered.

To learn of raptor migration junctures and established hawkwatches in your area, consider joining the Hawk Migration Association of North America (HMANA) (see page 130 for more information). HMANA's biannual journal, *Hawk Migration Studies*, gives details and seasonal counts from virtually all watch sites, well known and obscure, throughout the United States and Canada. Special features include identification articles, research, history, whimsy and news of conferences, workshops and raptor programs. Perhaps most important for the new hawkwatcher, HMANA has fliers about watch sites, large and small, throughout the continent. For example, HMANA's brochure for the "Northeast Region" (which includes Massachusetts, Rhode Island, Connecticut and parts of New York) describes the Lighthouse Point, New

Site listings from the Hawk Migration Association may lead you to an American kestrel.

Haven, Connecticut, hawkwatch in this way:

"Most productive of the coastal lookouts. Good for sharp-shins, kestrels, ospreys and harriers. Flights mainly in the morning. To reach the lookout from the west, take I-95 to exit 50. At the second stoplight turn right onto Townsend Avenue. Proceed a little over 2 miles, passing Morris Cove (part of New Haven harbor) on your right, to a stoplight. Turn right and go about a mile to Lighthouse Point Park entrance; drive into the park and look for hawkwatchers. Manned September 1 through October."

HMANA regional fliers will guide you to sites such as Militia Hill (just outside Philadelphia) and Sandy Hook, New Jersey (near New York City) where up to 8,000 hawks are seen in spring. Other pamphlets will help you find the Fire Island Hawkwatch on Long Island, New York, or even the Pelham Bay Watch, right in New York City. You'll have access to the fall watch at Concordia College on the shores of Lake Michigan (north of Milwaukee) or the site at Rockfish Gap in the Blue Ridge Mountains.

Learn From the Experts

IF YOU ARE NEW TO hawk migration watching, learn from the experienced. Follow directions to established watch sites and spend time with the regulars. Most watchers are happy to assist newcomers with spotting and identification. Sites such as Hawk Mountain and Cape May have interns on the watch during peak hours and peak season to help novices.

One final hint—if you journey to a watch site far from home, give yourself plenty of time there. Be prepared to wait for the "good front."

Hawk counter Frank Nicoletti at work at Braddock Bay, scanning clouds for high-flying raptors.

When asked about Cape May, we always recommend coming for at least a week—this should be enough time to guarantee a good flight or two. Twice we have gone to Braddock Bay, spending three days there each time. All six days it poured rain, and we saw a total of one northern harrier. On the first trip, Frank Nicoletti sounded the classic "Gosh, you should have been here yesterday." When we arrived home after the second trip, Jeff Dodge called to tell us, "Two days after you left, the warm front came through, the rain stopped, it cleared, and hawks filled the sky." So if you go, give yourself an extended opportunity. The right weather, persistence and a little luck will result in a wonderful view of the drama of hawk migration.

PART TWO

Hawks and Eagles
of North America

Red-tailed Hawk

Buteo jamaicensis
Length: 19"
Wingspan: 49"

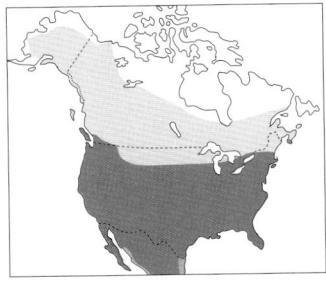

In all parts of North America except the far North, the red-tailed hawk is the raptor most often seen by birders and nonbirders alike.

Buteos, with their wide wings and soaring flight are the group that most laymen or beginning birders think of as the classic "hawk," and the red-tailed hawk is the quintessential buteo. It shares with the American kestrel the honor of being the most ubiquitous raptor in North America; these two raptors have the widest range of all the North American birds of prey.

Red-tailed hawks breed throughout the lower 48 states and north to the edge of tree-line in Alaska and the Canadian provinces except Labrador and Newfoundland. Besides being widespread geographically, they are undemanding in their choice of habitat. They nest in forests, woodlots and even remote tree-lines. In the West, nests might be placed in Saguaro cactuses or even on man-made structures. The red-tail's only real requirement is that its chosen home range have some open land—pasture, meadow, prairie, marsh or even arid brushland. It adapts to active agricultural lands quite well, as long as the farming doesn't eliminate all vestiges of natural habitat. With such cosmopolitan needs, red-tails are found from Vermont valley pastures to Ohio wood-lots, Alberta alpine meadows to Point Reyes Pacific Coast grasslands and south to border-land scrub. In terms of their adaptability, they are the most successful raptor in North America, and populations are healthy in virtually all regions. They are the easiest raptor to spot, everyone's common "roadside" hawk, found perched along interstate medians and rural farm roads.

Red-tails hunt from perches and aerial "platforms" by hovering and kiting. As are all buteos, they are consummate soarers. As opportunists, red-tails take a wide variety of prey. We have seen them prey on squirrels, rabbits, snakes, birds—even swimming muskrats. We witnessed one adult red-tailed hawk pluck a laughing gull from the same thermal in which they were both soaring. In the Midwest, some seem to specialize in hazing winter blackbird flocks. Mice and rats, however, are the prey items most commonly taken. Red-tails winter north to the line of deep, permanent snow cover.

While not a true long-distance migrant, with few leaving the U.S. in fall, the red-tail is nonetheless a migrant. For some, raptor migration is defined by swirling September broad-wings, but an equal number of birders do not feel that fall has really come until they see stocky red-tails bolting down eastern mountain ridges in howling November cold front gales. Red-tails are late-season staples of migration at fall localities like Hawk Mountain, Pennsylvania, and Duluth, Minnesota. They are early spring migrants at hawkwatch sites like Whitefish Point, Michigan, and Braddock Bay, New York, where they may appear as early as late February. A thousand birds per day is the sought-after legendary number in red-tail sightings, but many top spots may have a peak flight of 500 or more most seasons. Duluth holds the record, where an unbelievable 4,000-plus red-tails were carefully counted by Frank Nicoletti one red-letter October day.

Red-tails are not hard to spot; a day afield in any season almost anywhere on the continent should produce a sighting or two. Look for perched birds early in the day and soaring birds in midday if it is sunny. Search for their prominent silhouettes on the edge of open areas, fields, prairie, marsh and meadow. Aside from the aforementioned migration gatherings, our favorite places for red-tails include the southern Great Plains in winter, where the excellent national wildlife refuges of Kansas, Oklahoma and northern Texas attract numerous red-tails. In the Midwest and West, red-tails come in several subspecies and in a variety of color forms. The common western subspecies, *calurus*, has light, dark and even rufous forms. (Many older books use the word "phase," i.e. "dark-phase red-tail," and some newer books refer to this as the "dark morph." We prefer the term "form," because both "phase" and "morph" imply change. Neither red-tails, nor any raptors, ever change their color. A dark-form bird is born dark and remains dark throughout the many molts of its life span.) It is a challenge for the raptor spotter to identify all the

Practically ubiquitous in the U.S., the red-tailed hawk is what most birders think of as the "classic" hawk.

races or subspecies of red-tailed hawks. Look for the very pale race, the Krider's red-tailed hawk, on the northern Great Plains in sum-

Soaring red-tails can be identified by their white chest and belly, dark belly-band and dark comma near the wing tip.

mer and along the Gulf Coast states in winter. The uncommon dark northern Harlan's red-tailed hawk is rarely seen on its Alaskan breeding grounds but can usually be found at Squaw Creek NWR in Missouri, for example, in the winter months. Also try Salt Plains NWR in Oklahoma and Holla Bend, Arkansas, in winter for this striking bird, extolled as the "black warrior" by J.J. Audubon.

Other favorite red-tail spots include the Sulphur Springs Valley in southeastern Arizona, where the pale-bellied southwestern race, the Fuertes red-tail, is common, as well as a wide variety of other subspecies and plumages. The Texas coast in winter offers a plethora of red-tails, as does southern California's Antelope Valley. One of our premier sites will always be Cape May, New Jersey. It may be best-known for falcons and accipiters, but almost every year, on some halcyon mid-November day, red-tails converge over the Cape, usually after several days of prevailing northwest winds. It is then that our favorite kettles form, when we have seen 60 red-tails and 40 red-shoulders thermaling together.

Red-tails, with their distinctive buteo shape and easily seen field marks, are usually easy to identify. They soar on wide, flat or slightly raised wings. From below, light-form birds show a patch in the shape of a comma near the wing tips, a dark leading edge to the wing (the "patagial mark") and most (but not all) show a dark belly-band on an otherwise very pale belly. Adults have a brick-red upper tail, and young birds have a warm-brown banded tail. Even after you have spotted many red-tails, continue to search for them, for it is the species to which all others are compared when making identifications in the field.

How to Spot Hawks & Eagles

Red-shouldered Hawk

Buteo lineatus
Length: 17"
Wingspan: 40"

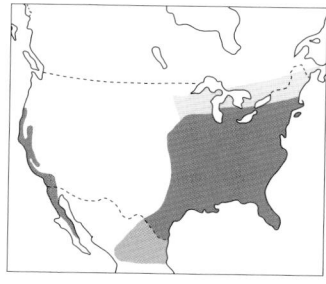

Except for a population found in coastal California, the red-shouldered hawk is decidedly an easterner, occupying a range that stretches from Florida and southern Texas, north to Michigan and Maine. It is found north of the Canadian border only in southeastern Ontario and extreme southern Quebec and New Brunswick. This medium-sized buteo inhabits deep, usually wet woodlands in the North and southern swamp forests from coastal New Jersey to Florida and the Gulf Coast. Red-shoulders can be locally common in parts of their range and scarce or absent, even in suitable habitat, in others. Only in the Deep South are they common to abundant, where they may be more common than red-tails.

Although quite secretive and a bird of remote forests in the North, in the South it is often trusting or even tame. In Everglades National Park, we have on occasion inadvertently walked to within a few feet of perched red-shoulders. Because of its secretive nature, the red-shoulder is often first detected by its strident calls, which pierce the morning air from the Maine woods to Corkscrew Swamp in Florida. It is particularly vocal, in fact often noisy, in the breeding season—whether announcing its territory, harassing potential predators or interlopers, or performing courtship flights over the canopy.

Compared to the red-tail, the red-shoulder is much more a bird of the forest. It often soars above woods and meadows, but usually hunts within the forest from perches, searching for reptiles and amphibians in summer, and mice, voles and shrews in winter.

The red-shoulder is migratory, retiring from northern forests in late fall in order to escape winter snows. It is an early migrant in spring, returning north with March thaws to reclaim its breeding territory. From the mid-Atlantic south, it is far less migratory; migra-

A bird of the forest, the red-shoulder is distinguished by its rufous shoulder patches.

tion there is mostly confined to the dispersing young of the year. In Florida, Texas and California, it is nonmigratory, resident throughout the year.

Especially vocal in the breeding season, the red-shouldered hawk is likely to be heard before it can be seen.

Migrant red-shoulders are late fall regulars at ridge hawkwatch sites such as Hawk Mountain in Pennsylvania. They don't fight the wind like red-tails, but mostly move on less windy days. Only at Great Lakes sites such as Braddock Bay and Derby Hill, both in New York, can red-shoulders be considered abundant migrants. At Braddock, up to 1,400 have been counted in a day during late March warm fronts, all adults heading north with the spring. At most other migration sites, they are regular but never abundant. At Cape May, they number about 500 per fall (compared to about 2,000 red-tails).

Sure sites for spotting red-shoulders include state parks and state wildlife management areas almost anywhere in Florida. They are a common roadside bird in the Everglades, often sitting on telephone poles and wires. Try Myakka River State Park or National Audubon's Corkscrew Swamp Sanctuary. In Texas, they are common in the bottomlands of the Big Thicket National Preserve. California red-shoulders are fairly easy to spot between Santa Barbara and the San Francisco Bay area.

Adult red-shouldered hawks are easily identified by their rich reddish or barred breast and bold black and white banded tail and flight feathers. On perched birds seen from the back, the red shoulders should be readily visible. Young birds have a streaked chest, unlike the red-tail's white chest with a belly-band. The red-shoulder soars on flat wings that are thrust slightly forward (unlike the red-tail and broad-wing, which hold their wings straight out, perpendicular to the body), and the tail is long for a buteo. Red-shoulders always show a translucent crescent-shaped "window" in the outer wing at the base of the primaries. Red-shoulder subspecies are identifiable, with Florida birds being much paler below and grayish above, and California birds showing rich rufous tones below.

Wherever found, the red-shoulder is a handsome bird, thought by many to be the most beautiful hawk in North America.

84

Broad-winged Hawk

Buteo platypterus
Length: 15"
Wingspan: 34"

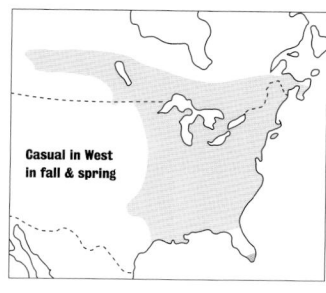

Casual in West
in fall & spring

Kettling in surging, boiling masses and flowing over hawkwatches in vast squadrons, the legions of broad-wings coursing north with the spring and south with the fall define raptor migration and gave rise to the sport of hawk-watching. The annual flight of broad-winged hawks from Canada and eastern U.S. forests to the mountain forests of Central and South America and back is one of the great migration spectacles on the planet, with few equals in drama and wonder.

The broad-winged hawk is the smallest of the common buteos, yet one of the most amazing fliers. It is probably the most dependent of all hawks on thermals. Riding columns and rivers of air many thousands of miles each year, broad-wings travel as far as Chile and Argentina for the winter. Like the red-shoulder, the broad-wing is a forest buteo, breeding and raising its young in deciduous or mixed woodlands from New Brunswick west to Alberta and south to Georgia and Louisiana. It is an easterner, breeding almost wholly east of the 100th meridian (or the Great Plains) except in the far North. Their weak but pleasant whistling call carries well through northern forests on hot, humid summer days. A common bird of the North, broad-wings are scarce-to-rare breeders in the southern parts of their range. In many mid-Atlantic areas, they are thought to be declining along with the reptiles and amphibians on which they commonly feed—frogs, toads and snakes. They also catch small mammals, birds and insects. Because of their food preferences, broad-wings arrive late in the spring and depart early in the fall. Except for a very few that winter in southern Florida, broad-wings are absent from the U.S. in winter.

One of the smallest buteos, the broad-wing travels many thousands of miles each year.

Spotting broad-wings can be a feast or famine proposition. Shy and inconspicuous during the breeding season, even where common in northern forests, they form enormous flocks during migration. Although easily seen then, they frustrate hawkwatchers with their tendency to form huge kettles and narrow "streams," or glide paths. Few birders are satisfied with 400 broad-wings when they hear later that two ridges over, just 15 miles away, 10,000 broad-wings were tallied in a two-hour period.

During migration, broad-winged hawks are easily seen in hundreds of places across the continent. You can't miss at Santa Ana NWR or Bentsen-Rio Grande Valley State Park in Texas in late March or early April. Also in spring, hitting the right front at Whitefish Point in Michigan or Braddock Bay in New York in late April should place you in the midst of a highly memorable flight. During mid-September cold fronts, best spots include Lake Erie Metropark near the mouth of the Detroit River in Michigan, Hawk Ridge at Duluth in Minnesota and Hawk Mountain in Pennsylvania. A week at Hazel Bazemore County Park in Corpus Christi, Texas, in late September should probably allow you to see about 100,000 broad-wings. Although rare on the West Coast, broad-wings are recorded annually at Golden Gate in

Many broad-wings winter in the mountain cloud forests of Venezuela, South America, *top*. Shy during the breeding season, *bottom*, broad-wings form enormous flocks, or "kettles," during migration flights.

California. Usually just 50 to 250 birds are seen, but they always include a few of the rare dark-form broad-wings from the far western

How to Spot Hawks & Eagles

portion of the broad-winged hawk's breeding range in Alberta.

Our own favorite broad-wing sightings include watching a few flapping down the main street of Key West in Florida on a blustery January day and seeing several trans-Gulf migrants over the Dry Tortugas in late April, soaring with brown pelicans and magnificent frigatebirds. Our most poignant sighting was three broad-wings soaring over the cloud forest peaks of Henri Pittier National Park in Venezuela on a hot southern summer day in February. These neotropical migrants share the Venezuelan forests with green honeycreepers and blue-winged mountain-tanagers, and the skies with black and white hawk-eagles and solitary eagles. It seemed special to see "our" broad-wings from back home spending the winter in the tropics, and it helped us realize that broad-wing conservation only just begins at home.

To identify broad-wings, remember that the wings are not noticeably broad. Compare adult broad-wing plumage to that of a redshoulder. A broad-wing's barring is more chestnut in color and the tail bands are fewer and bolder. Immature broad-wings are variable, from pale and lightly streaked to heavily streaked below. The underwings are pale compared to other species. For a buteo, broadwings have particularly pointed wings—the outer portion of the wing is swept back while soaring, giving the wing a candleflame-like shape. They glide with gentle swept-back wings and both glide and soar with wings slightly drooped below the body. Their flight is buoyant and agile, and broad-wings can gain altitude remarkably rapidly in a thermal.

Swainson's Hawk

Buteo swainsoni
Length: 19½"
Wingspan: 51"

Casual
in East
in fall &
spring

If one considers the broad-winged hawk an easterner, then the Swainson's hawk is a westerner. And because the Swainson's hawk is a bird of open plains, prairies and grasslands, there is very little or no overlap in the ranges of broad-wings and Swainson's. When you head west and run out of trees, the Swainson's hawk replaces the broad-wing as the common buteo.

Swainson's hawks nest north into central Alaska and the Yukon, south to Mexico, and almost completely west of the 100th meridian. They winter on the Argentine pampas. Forming huge flocks for migration, they are one of the longest-distance migrants of any raptor. Because of the large flocks and their thermaling behavior, migration counts vary considerably from year to year at given sites. In fall, the Goshutes in Nevada record between 35 and 350, and the Manzano Mountain count in New Mexico has varied from 9 to 7,300 depending on the route the flocks travel. South Texas is *the* place to see Swainson's hawks in fall—counts there vary from 10,000 to 50,000 most seasons. A few wander east each fall: Duluth records 3 to 11 each year; Cape May 2 to 7. Over 100 are stranded in South Florida each fall, and many successfully overwinter there. The only other known wintering locale in the U.S. is in California's Sacramento-San Joaquin River delta, where about 30 Swainson's hawks have been found each winter in recent years.

Swainson's hawks have a varied diet and might be encountered on the ground searching for insects and earthworms in recently plowed fields , kiting and hovering in search of rodents, or hawking dragonflies on high. For a buteo, their wings are long and have very pointed tips, seen as they soar and glide with a noticeable dihedral (a V shape). The Swainson's hawk is the most variable in coloration of all North American raptors—there are light forms and dark forms and a variety of intergrades. Whether part of a high flock over Bentsen-Rio Grande Valley State Park or a single vagrant over an eastern ridge, this high-plains drifter is always an exciting find.

Rough-legged Hawk

Buteo lagopus
Length: 24"
Wingspan: 56"

The rough-legged hawk is a summer resident of the high Arctic, nesting from Alaska to Labrador on rocky cliffs rising out of the tundra. To escape the frozen northern winter, they migrate to the lower 48 states each fall and spend the winter in open areas, including farmlands, marshes and grasslands. For most of us, they remain an enigma. While we long to see rough-legs in summer on their tundra river bluffs, most raptor spotters must be satisfied with finding them in their winter haunts on the New England coastal marshes, open country bordering the Great Lakes or farm country in the Pacific Northwest. Even then, they are rarely common, and we know of no one who has seen their fill of these Arctic wanderers.

Rough-legged hawk numbers vary from winter to winter. Their breeding success is controlled by the availability of small rodents, primarily lemmings, during the lengthy days of the brief Arctic summer. When the lemming population is high, there will be large broods. Rough-legs eat rodents almost exclusively; reflecting this, its talons are smaller and feet less powerful than those of the red-

A soaring light form Swainson's displays its light wing linings and dark flight feathers.

tail (which takes a wider variety of prey).

In part because of uneven breeding success, the rough-leg is an irruptive migrant and wintering bird, with numbers and food supply combining to create boom or bust numbers south of their breeding range. Rough-legs come late in the fall migration, peaking in November at both Duluth and Hawk Mountain. Duluth holds the fall rough-leg crown with over 1,000 seen there during fall 1994. About 400 to 500 is a normal season average. And because their Arctic breeding grounds remain snow covered late into the spring, they are late spring migrants, peaking in late April at Whitefish Point in Michigan. Whitefish is a prime site to spot rough-legs, with over 1,200 seen there on springs following irruptive flights. Both Derby Hill and Braddock Bay in New York are excellent, too, with over 500 sighted most years.

Vole population explosions attract winter aggregations. Owl invasions get most of the press, but areas with good concentrations of short-eared and snowy owls usually hold numerous rough-legs as well. We have seen good winter gatherings at Amherst Island, Ontario, and Point Peninsula in northeastern New York State near Watertown. The Duluth area sometimes holds good numbers of rough-legs in winter, with up to 100 recorded on the Christmas Bird Count there. Normally though, the raptor spotter should be satisfied with two or three a day in winter.

Rough-legs are rare south of the Delmarva Peninsula in the East and rarely reach south of central Texas in the West. The Tule Lake area of California and the Skagit Flats of Washington are excellent for rough-legs in winter.

Rough-leg plumage varies considerably. The light form, *above*, is more common.

Two of our favorite spots are the Pennsylvania Dutch farmlands near Lancaster, Pennsylvania, where hay fields and "old-fashioned" farming practices leave plenty behind for rodents and birds, and the shores of the Delaware Bay, where we once saw 30 rough-legs on a memorable December day near Money Island in Cumberland County, New Jersey.

Rough-legs are large, long-tailed and long-winged buteos. While they are slightly larger than red-tails, they are slighter in build, and their long, narrower wings give them a rangier look. They hover and kite like red-tails, the only other buteo in the East to do so. They soar with the wings held above the body in a dihedral, but not as much as a turkey vulture.

Rough-legs have a variety of plumages. Dark-form birds can look much like turkey vultures with blackish feathering below contrasting with silvery flight feathers. Among light-form rough-legs, immatures show black belly-bands (more so than red-tails) and black "carpal patches" on the underwing at the base of the primaries. Adults are less boldly patterned, with both the belly-band and carpal patches muted through mottling. All should show some variation of a white tail with a dark tip. (Clark and Wheeler's *Hawks* is an excellent reference for the intricacies of rough-leg and other raptor plumage variations—see page 129.) In the East, about one in four rough-legs is a dark form, but dark forms are far less common in the West. In any plumage, the rough-legged hawk is a prize for the raptor spotter.

Ferruginous Hawk

Buteo regalis
Length: 24"
Wingspan: 57"

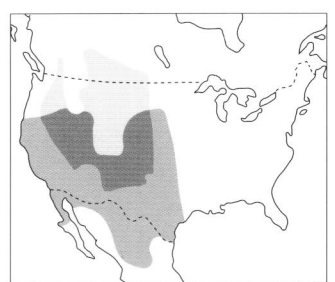

The ferruginous hawk is the largest buteo in North America and a bird of western open spaces. They breed from south-

Pale below with rusty back and shoulders, the ferruginous hawk is the largest buteo.

ern Alberta and Saskatchewan south to northern Texas and New Mexico and withdraw to California, Arizona and south into Mexico in winter. Nowhere are they particularly numerous, and they are a species of special concern to raptor conservationists, far rarer than bald eagles. Being relatively short-distance migrants, only a few are seen at established migration watches. Twenty to thirty are seen each fall at Golden Gate (California), the Goshutes (Nevada) and the Wellsvilles (Utah), and 10 to 20 each spring in the Sandias (New Mexico). For best accessibility, look for summer breeding ferruginous hawks at the Snake River Birds of Prey area near Boise, Idaho. Wintering birds can be seen from Attwater Prairie Chicken NWR, just west of Houston, Texas, west through Oklahoma and into New Mexico, Arizona and California. The Sulphur Springs Valley, south of Willcox, Arizona, is a sure bet. In California, the Antelope Valley and Carizzo Plain are two of the better winter areas.

Ferruginous hawks, seen almost exclusively in the West, are the largest buteos in North America.

To identify ferruginous hawks, look for a large buteo with a rusty back and shoulders above. They are very pale below, with rusty leg feathers (on adults only). In flight, they soar with a dihedral and show bright white upperwing patches on the outer portion of the wing and a pale whitish tail. There is a dark form, but fewer than one in ten are dark. Although there is some variation, there are no true intermediate forms. The ferruginous hawk's wing flap is heavy, like that of an eagle. They hunt in a similar manner to golden eagles, working hill crests for prairie dogs and chasing down jackrabbits. Some biologists feel that due to their structure and behavior, they may indeed be more closely related to golden eagles than to other buteos.

Like eagles, ferruginous hawks and many other hawks are still persecuted, often in indirect ways. At Muleshoe NWR in the Texas panhandle, we watched refuge personnel poisoning prairie dog colonies in response to grazing-interest pressures. Overhead, five ferruginous hawks circled, unaware that soon there would be nothing to eat there during the coming bitter north Texas winter.

Sharp-shinned Hawk

Accipiter striatus
Length: 11"
Wingspan: 23"

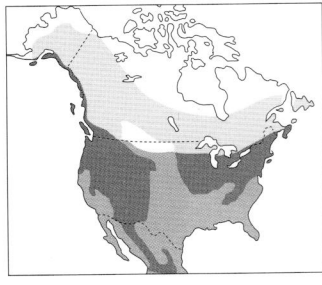

It was a big flight, a *big* flight, and Pete Dunne had been too busy to say much. The sound of the clickers had been saying it all, and they had been working overtime as Pete recorded the passage of each bird down the treeline. His only comments had been in pointing out the occasional diversion: "male harrier over the dunes," "young shoulder over the smoke stack." Finally, Pete lowered his binoculars. "Clay," he said tentatively, "you may not believe this, and I'm not sure I do either, but I just had over 1,000 sharp-shins during that last scan." Incredulous, Clay scanned against the tide of moving hawks, working up to the Magnesite Plant, and then east towards Cape May. The flowing wave of sharp-shins was continuous, and soon he resorted to counting the birds in blocks of 10's, "420, 430, 440 . . ." By the time he got to 950, Clay had to admit Pete was right. That early October day had produced a flight for the record books. Subsequent flights have been wondrous in their own right, but we've never again seen 1,000 sharp-shins at once.

Accipiters are furtive forest-dwelling hawks during the breeding season, but mainstays at migration viewing sites when passage birds flood the coasts and ridges during spring and fall. Sharp-shinned hawks are the smallest accipiter and breed to the limits of treeline from Alaska east to Newfoundland. They winter from the northern U.S. (farther north along the coasts) south to Central America, Cuba and the West Indies. They live and hunt in wooded areas; their only prey is small birds. Warblers and sparrows are the primary prey, but they will take birds as large as starlings and blackbirds, and we once saw a sharp-shin attack a blue jay (a bird about their own size). They hunt from perches, singling out a vic-

The smallest of the accipiters, sharp-shins may prey on birds as large as blue jays.

A banding demonstration compares the sizes of the sharp-shin, *left*, and the Cooper's, *right*.

tim (often a sick or injured songbird in a flock) and catching it after a brief rapid chase, or they course through the woods and hedgerows hoping to surprise prey. Like most accipiters, sharp-shins have stubby, rounded wings and a long rudder-like tail. Their migration flight is very distinctive: flap, flap, flap, then glide. At coastal migration junctures, they sometimes form loose kettles of 30 to 40 birds, and they soar well, often to great heights.

Sharp-shins migrate throughout the fall, but there is a clear pattern of young birds moving first, in September and early October in most places, with adults coming later in October and early November. They are ubiquitous: Golden Gate in California gets up to 5,000 each fall, the Goshutes about 1,500. Duluth, Minnesota, may record up to 20,000; Hawk Mountain up to 12,000. Cape May is the champ with an amazing 61,000 counted during the autumn of 1984 (although 30,000 is more the average). In spring, Derby Hill and Whitefish Point each record 8,000 to 10,000 or so. Flights have declined in the East in the past decade. Reasons offered for this downturn run from the effects of weather patterns, to habitat loss and alteration on the breeding grounds, to loss of songbird prey from tropical deforestation. Other theories counter with the possibility that a much larger portion of the population is remaining in the North (not migrating as far), benefitting from increased bird feeding and burgeoning house finch populations. It is even possible that sharp-shin populations are cyclical to an unknown degree.

Although shy and secretive in the breeding season, few specific recommendations are needed for finding migrant sharp-shins. The East Coast is best, and we have enjoyed northbound sharp-shins zipping through the dunes at Sandy Hook, New Jersey, in spring and southbound birds at Cape Hatteras in fall. We have been particularly intrigued by sharp-shins flapping low through the waves of the Gulf Stream in the Florida Straits in April, resolutely returning to their northern forest homes after a winter sojourn in Cuba or the West Indies.

Cooper's Hawk
Accipiter cooperii
Length: 16½"
Wingspan: 31"

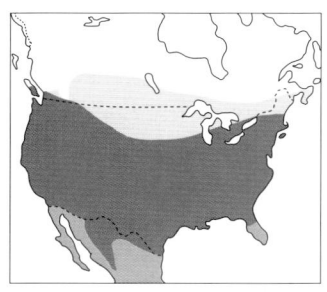

The Cooper's hawk is the medium-sized accipiter of North America, a crow-sized bird that breeds across southern Canada and most of the United States in open deciduous or mixed woodlands. The Cooper's is a ghost of the northern forest and the wraith of southwestern canyonlands. It can be remarkably secretive during the breeding season even where numerous, and many views are restricted to brief glimpses of birds passing silently through forest glades. Only on migration is it highly visible and often numerous.

Although the Cooper's preferred prey is birds, in the West they take lizards and ground squirrels, and some easterners specialize in chipmunks and even red squirrels. Cooper's hawks become aggressive and lose their shyness when hunting barnyards and yards with bird feeders. The Cooper's is probably the bird most responsible for the "chicken hawk" moniker and reputation, and they indeed can make quick work of unprotected chickens. Normal prey, however, are birds the size of grackles, jays and flickers. We once watched a Cooper's hawk walk around a fallow field looking under bushes for "frozen" bobwhite quail; it successfully pounced on the first one that flushed. We also once saw a female Cooper's stoop on a wood duck flushed by our canoe, the outcome a mystery as they disappeared in tandem around a bend in the tidal creek.

The Cooper's hawk was a classic victim of DDT poisoning, and their numbers plummeted in the 1960s. They are recovering well in recent years. In New Jersey, a nest we found in 1987 was the first in the South Jersey region in 50 years, but by 1995, nearly 40 pairs had been discovered by breeding bird atlasers. Migration counts continue to grow throughout the East.

While sharp-shins virtually always outnumber Cooper's hawks during migration, there are many areas of the country where the Cooper's is a far more common breeder. This is particularly true in the West, where it is a regular nester in streamside woodlands and open forests. During migration, the Cooper's is a soaring hawk, depending more on thermals and less on flapping flight than sharp-shins. At Kiptopeke, Virginia, for example, windy days bring hundreds of sharp-shins and

Cooper's hawks hunt from perches, often singling out a sick or injured songbird at a backyard feeder.

see between 500 and 1,000. Up to 2,700 pass over Cape May each autumn.

Much has been written about accipiter identification, and it remains a fact that separating sharp-shinned hawks from Cooper's hawks is one of the hardest tasks facing hawk-watchers on a daily basis. It is complicated by the fact that there is a considerable size difference between males and females of each species, with males often noticeably smaller. Remember, wingspans given here are averages, and a male sharp-shin might range from 20 to 22 inches and a female from 23 to 26. A male Cooper's hawk wingspan may be 28 to 30 inches and a female 31 to 34. So, while large female sharp-shins are always larger than small male Cooper's, the two-inch difference is hardly discernable under field conditions. For identification, concentrate on shape. A sharp-shin is small headed with a squared off tail. Cooper's hawks have a larger protruding head and a rounded, more plume-like tail. Soaring Cooper's hawks show a straight leading edge to the wing (think of them as looking like a flying cross), where the leading edge of a sharp-shinned hawk's wing shows a slight curve. Adults of both species are gray above, with warm, rusty barring below. Young birds of each species are streaked below, but Cooper's much more sparsely on the lower belly, giving them a dark-headed, hooded look. Don't despair with accipiter ID, most veterans admit that some defy ID because of a mixture of field marks. A few days spent at a migration hotspot can go a long way toward helping with those brief glimpses back home of clandestine accipiters stealing through the summer woodlands.

few if any Cooper's. With moderating winds and temperatures the following day, Cooper's might outnumber sharp-shins as they circle high on thermals over the Cape Charles islands and tidal wetlands.

Cooper's are an integral part of western mountain migration counts, with up to 1,700 seen in a fall season at the Goshutes in Nevada. Golden Gate in California gets up to 2,500 on the Pacific route. During the spring season, Braddock Bay, New York, may

Northern Goshawk

Accipiter gentilis
Length: 21"
Wingspan: 41"

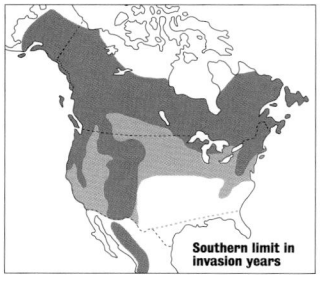

It only happens on a major scale about every ten years, but an invasion of northern goshawks may be the singular event that hawk-watchers await. When the low points of the cyclical populations of snowshoe hares and ruffed grouse coincide, goshawks, the largest of our accipiters, move south en masse in search of food, leaving boreal forests and fanning out into the fields and forests of the lower 48 states.

The goshawk is a northern breeder from the limits of treeline across Alaska and Canada, east through New England and south through the Appalachian Mountains. In the West, it nests in the mountains of California and south through the Rockies into the coniferous sky islands of southern Arizona. Most years, many adults are either nonmigratory or short-distance migrants, with only the young dispersing south. In the West there is an annual altitudinal migration with birds descending to lower elevations each winter. During invasion years, adults and young migrate and show up far to the south of their normal range.

Although the goshawk is a consummate forest raptor, flight years will take them far out of habitat, and they may appear in farmland, woodlots or on the edges of coastal marshes.

The name "goshawk" is an Anglo-Saxon derivative of goose hawk, and although a goshawk could and possibly does take small geese, it normally feeds on prey the size of grouse and pheasants. In many areas, goshawks take mostly mammals, such as squirrels and rabbits. They are highly aggressive. There is an old tale of a goshawk flying right into a farmhouse kitchen chasing a chicken. At Cape May, we have seen young goshawks resolutely chase pigeons round and round the bunker on the beach and stoop on waterfowl on Lily Lake, sending the neighborhood into turmoil. They are fierce and relentless in their nest defense, and we have had to hit the ground and back rapidly away when unknowingly coming upon a goshawk nest during a survey of an Appalachian forest.

Goshawks are highly aggressive, often capturing pigeons, grouse or pheasants.

On northern forest breeding grounds, goshawks are most often seen over the trees, carrying prey to nest and nestlings. On migration, look for them late in the season. They are scarce but expected at Hawk Mountain—the second week of November is best—with about 100 seen per year. In the Goshutes, up to 150 are seen; they usually peak the second week of October. Duluth has the best goshawk flights on the continent. Numbers are highly variable, from just several hundred on a "nonflight" season to nearly 6,000 a fall on a major "invasion year." In winter, look for goshawks perched on lower branches in sunlit forest edges early in the morning, a rare but exciting find.

Crows dislike goshawks with a level of hatred normally reserved only for great horned owls. Alarm calls of crows, jays and magpies may alert you to a goshawk. We watched one memorable Arizona Apache goshawk (southwestern subspecies) flying down Ramsey Canyon. The alarm calls of elegant trogons gave its presence away even after it was long out of sight in the mountain forest dusk.

The northern goshawk is a very buteo-like accipiter more likely to be confused with a red-shouldered hawk than a Cooper's hawk. It is large—females can be the size of a red-tailed hawk. The gray-backed plumage of adults should be easily recognizable, and the black eye patch is prominent. Young goshawks are variable, but generally more tawny in color and more heavily streaked than young Cooper's hawks. In a soar, their shape looks more like the sharp-shin, with curved leading and trailing edges to the wings, than like the Cooper's hawk.

American Kestrel

Falco sparverius
Length: 9½"
Wingspan: 21½"

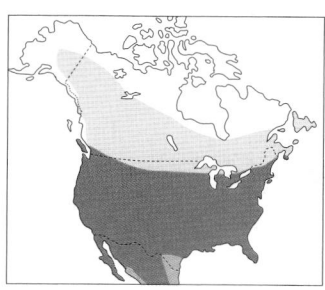

The American kestrel is the smallest of the North American falcons and the one most commonly spotted. Like all falcons, it is a bird of open country. Its shrill "killy, killy, killy" call can be heard over farms, grasslands, meadow, desert and open woodlands. It perches on fences, utility wires and poles with its tail constantly bobbing, and often hovers motionless—except for rapidly beating wings—as it

Kestrels readily use nest boxes if suitable hunting habitat is available nearby.

scans for insects, lizards or rodents. Once known as the sparrow hawk, it will occasionally take small birds. They are sexually dimorphic—males show a brick red tail and slate blue-gray upperwings, while females have warm-brown barred wings and tails. Kestrels nest in tree cavities, but also readily use holes in banks and cliffs and crevices in buildings and barns. They can be fairly common in cities and towns if farmland is nearby. They readily use nest boxes and can be attracted if suitable hunting habitat is available. In some areas of the East, the American kestrel is thought to be declining in numbers, possibly a victim of modern intensive and sterile agricultural practices and/or the loss of farmland.

Kestrel are widespread across North America in open country, found everywhere except northern Alaska and northernmost Canada. They are highly migratory, spreading throughout the southern United States in winter, many entering Mexico. Although conspicuous and easily spotted in both summer and winter, it is during the fall migration that they become abundant in coastal areas. Up to 700 have been seen in a season at Golden Gate, California. Holiday Beach, Ontario, flights average about 3,000. Cape May averages about 12,000 each fall. Once, on October 16, 1970, 24,875 kestrel were estimated flying past the Cape May Lighthouse in a single day, a "back up" of birds following a long period of bad weather and poor migratory conditions.

Normally, September is the peak month at

The male kestrel is distinguished by its brick red tail and slate blue-gray upperwings.

all fall migratory junctures. The first and second weeks of April are best in spring, but spring flights are more geographically widespread. Sandy Hook, New Jersey, gets about 2,500 each spring; Whitefish Point, Michigan, up to 800.

Merlin

Falco columbarius
Length: 10½"
Wingspan: 24"

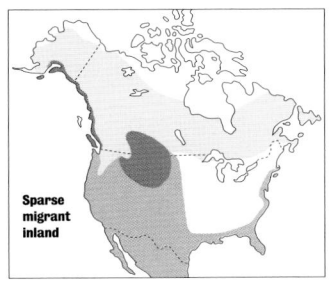

Sparse migrant inland

As the sun lowered in the late October sky and the ocean turned that rich cobalt blue that only afternoon light can impart, Clay noticed the merlin coming up the beach—a hunting merlin, not like the several migrants he had seen heading south down the coastal strand while surf fishing that day. The dark little falcon accelerated, pumping hard just a foot over the sand at water's edge. The flock of sanderling flushed, all twisting and turning, wheeling together for protection. As the merlin burst through the flock, one sanderling turned the wrong way and was singled out from the protection of the flock. It flew hard out over the ocean, then turned back over the dunes; the merlin was rarely more than a few feet from its tail. The merlin attempted to tire the sandpiper, to fly it down in classic merlin fashion.

The sanderling flock was already feeding again, probing at water's edge as the drama played out above them. For five minutes the chase went on. The merlin tried several times to gain enough altitude for a stoop, giving up proximity for advantage, trading position for speed. As they passed within a few yards, Clay wondered if the sanderling felt terror. The birds passed out of sight behind a dune to the north, the outcome a mystery. About a half-hour later, in the gathering dusk, Clay saw a

Renowned for its low, very fast flight, the merlin can be spotted in good numbers each fall along the Atlantic Coast.

merlin flying leisurely over the surf. Noticing the bird's bulging crop, he now knew the outcome and felt remorse for the sanderling, even as he respected the merlin—life and death on a lonely coastal beach. As he headed for the car, the merlin, now perched across the inlet, preened, fluffed its feathers, then slept.

The merlin is a small falcon, with males no larger than a female kestrel. They nest on the tundra and in open boreal woodlands in Alaska and throughout Canada east to Nova Scotia, as well as in the mountains of Washington, Montana and Wyoming. They winter throughout the West, but usually only along the coast in the East. During migration, they are scarce inland in fall and only a bit more numerous and widespread in spring. The only place merlins can be regarded as common is on the Atlantic Coast in fall. At Fire Island on Long Island, New York, over 1,600 can be seen in the fall. Cape May or Kiptopeke might tally 3,000 each, and over 500 have been seen in a single day. Late September and the first half of October are best. Falcons are known for their afternoon migration, but merlins are notorious for late-afternoon flights. These coastal speed demons apparently feed during the mornings and migrate later in the day. Over the Cape May Point State Park marshes and dunes, "merlin madness" occurs during the afternoons and sometimes up until dusk as scores of these swift hunters pause during their migration to feed on dragonflies, tree swallows and even bats.

Formerly called "pigeon hawk," the merlin is neither pigeon-sized nor does it hunt pigeons. They are opportunistic, taking shorebirds and yellow-rumped warblers in the East and longspurs and horned larks over western grasslands. Merlins are dark in color compared to kestrels. Both sexes are heavily streaked with brown below; females are brown above and adult males (the "blue jacks") are slate-blue above. Merlins are best identified by their low, very fast flight, quite unlike the weaker, meandering flapping and gliding of kestrels. A merlin's wings are proportionately wider and stubbier than a kestrel's. Merlins are pugnacious—often harassing much larger birds. We once watched a migrating merlin repeatedly stoop on a golden eagle. A prize for the raptor spotter is the "prairie merlin," a pale race breeding in south central Canada and the northern prairie states. Easily identified in the field, adult males can appear pale powdery blue above, contrasting with tawny streaking below.

Peregrine Falcon
Falco peregrinus
Length: 16"
Wingspan: 41"

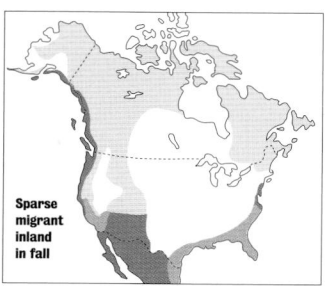

Sparse migrant inland in fall

Peregrines occur worldwide, are spectacular in their hunting flight and migrations and have long been fabled in literature. For the hawk aficionado, watching peregrines is a pure pleasure.

There are three recognizable races in North America. The pale Arctic race, the "tundra peregrine," breeds on cliffs rising above tundra

Peregrines are masterful fliers, "stooping" (flying down) on prey at speeds of 90 mph.

rivers in Alaska and the Yukon and across northern Canada. The dark coastal race, the Peale's peregrine, nests from British Columbia north to the Aleutian Islands and is mostly nonmigratory. The continental race breeds in canyonlands and mountains from central Alaska south through west Texas. In the East, the continental race (subspecies *anatum*) was extirpated through the ravages of DDT in the 1960s. Through reintroduction, peregrines in the East have slowly regained most of their former range and again nest on remote cliff faces in New England south through the Appalachians, as well as on bridges, buildings and artificial nesting towers along the coast.

Peregrines are masterful fliers well known for their spectacular stoops on prey. They eat birds almost exclusively. Male peregrines are smaller and take songbirds, jays and shorebirds. Females can take larger prey: shorebirds, ducks and even gulls. They were once aptly called duck hawks, as anyone who has seen peregrines hunting teal will attest. We once watched a mile-long stoop on a flying razorbill—the alcid literally flew into the water at

Peregrines nest on western cliff faces like these at Big Bend National Park in Texas.

the last millisecond, the splash soaking the pursuing peregrine. City peregrines ably take starlings and pigeons.

Peregrinus in Latin means "wandering" and aptly describes the peregrine's migrations. Tundra peregrines regularly migrate from Alaska, the Yukon and Greenland to South America. Males are particularly known for their overwater migration and are commonly seen in Bermuda, for example. Powerful fliers, while out over the ocean they feed in flight on petrel or doomed migrant songbirds that have been blown offshore. Peregrines are decidedly coastal in their fall migration. Each fall, Duluth, Minnesota, sees about 50, and Hawk Mountain, Pennsylvania, about 25, but over 1,100 have been recorded at Cape May. Similar numbers occur at Assateague in Maryland and Kiptopeke in Virginia. The Florida Keys are good as well. Padre Island in South Texas has seen up to 800 in fall and an amazing 1,250 in spring, as birds return north from Central and South America. In spring, birds fan out after leaving South Texas, following shorebirds north through the Great Plains, and no concentrations are seen. For example, only about 20 are recorded at Braddock Bay, New York, in spring. Continental breeders are far less migratory than tundra birds.

The Atlantic Coast in fall is a must for seeing peregrines, but some of our favorites remain the breeding birds we watched riding updrafts off steep canyon walls in Big Bend National Park, Texas, and one lilting along over the Atlantic Ocean about 50 miles off the Maryland coast near the Baltimore Canyon. On the vast llanos (savannas) of Venezuela, we have watched a number of wintering peregrines working the endless grasslands and plains, hunting such diverse prey as dickcissels, yellowlegs, southern lapwings and Brazilian ducks.

For identification, remember that peregrines are variable in size. Some males appear relatively small and some females look huge (wingspread can vary from as little as 37 inches in males to as large as 46 inches in females). Immatures appear dark like merlins, but adults appear light below (males are particularly white below). Tundra males are pale gray above, continental and Peale's birds are dark gray to black above. Peregrines are best identified by their powerful direct flight and rapid deep, yet flexible, whippy wing beats. Peregrines soar well, showing a distinctive pointed wing and spread tail shape, not unlike that of a gull. In hard glides or stoops, the wings are dramatically swept back.

Prairie Falcon

Falco mexicanus
Length: 16"
Wingspan: 40"

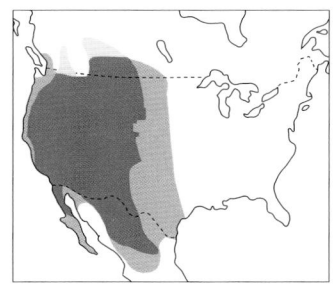

A relatively rare sighting at hawkwatches, the prairie falcon is a bird of open country.

The prairie falcon is a westerner, breeding from the Canadian plains south into northern Mexico. It is only a partial migrant, withdrawing from the northernmost nesting areas for the winter. Only a few are seen at hawkwatches—usually 30 to 40 in the Goshutes in fall and 24 to 30 in the Sandias in spring, mostly in March. A few wander east of their normal range each fall and winter. Prairie falcons are large falcons, only slightly smaller than peregrines, and are birds of open country—plains, prairie, grasslands and deserts. They nest on bluffs and cliffs. Unlike peregrines, prairie falcons favorite prey is small mammals—ground squirrels in particular—but they also take lizards, insects and even small birds (particularly in winter). Prairie falcons fly low and fast over open country, surprising their prey and chasing it down. They also soar well and sometimes stoop on their targets. Prairie falcons are paler in overall color than most peregrines and have a fainter facial pattern. They are brown-backed and faintly streaked below. In flight, look for the dark underwing coverts. Their wings are slightly less pointed than those of a peregrine, and their wingbeat is slightly stiffer.

Nowhere numerous, the prairie falcon should nonetheless be easily spotted in winter in the Sulphur Springs Valley in Arizona or in valley grasslands east of Reno, Nevada, near Fallon. California's Antelope Valley, Carizzo Plain and Cuyama Valley are reliable spots in winter. In summer, check bluffs in Pawnee National Grassland, Colorado. By far the most accessible place to spot prairie falcons is the Snake River Birds of Prey area near Boise, Idaho. There, their courtship flights, interactions with other raptors and low, bullet-like hunting flights can best be appreciated.

Another western raptor, the **aplomado falcon** (*Falco femoralis*), was once found in grasslands along the Mexican border from southeast Arizona to southeast Texas, but was extirpated by the 1950s. An intensive reintroduction program begun at Laguna Atascosa NWR in southern Texas in the 1990s has biologists guardedly optimistic, and at least one pair is now breeding in the wild. Drive the wildlife loop road at Laguna and scan exposed perches. Check the "hack tower" and ask at refuge headquarters for the latest sightings and/or information. Aplomados are slightly smaller and much darker above than prairie falcons. Look for a slate-gray-backed bird (adult) with a dark cummerbund.

Gyrfalcon

Falco rusticolus
Length: 22"
Wingspan: 48"

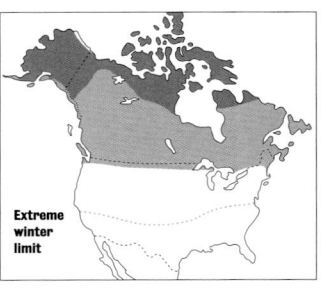

Extreme
winter
limit

The largest of all falcons and a rare winter visitor from the high Arctic, the gyrfalcon (pronounced "jeer-falcon") is the ultimate quest for raptor spotters, the rarest and hardest of all North American hawks to find. Unless you live in a remote village in the high Arctic, you must wait until the bitter winter prairie winds sweep the northern Great Plains to find a gyrfalcon, or brave the winter wind-swept icy coasts of Alaska, British Columbia or the Maritimes in search of this Holy Grail of raptor seekers.

The gyrfalcon is a large bird with a variety of color forms, from almost pure black to pure white. Gray birds are most common. They are circumpolar, nesting on Arctic tundra cliffs in some of the most barren and remote regions

A flying prairie falcon is distinguished from a peregrine by its dark underwing coverts.

The ultimate sighting for a raptor spotter, the gyrfalcon is a rare visitor from the Arctic.

on Earth. In summer, they prey upon a variety of Arctic nesting shorebirds and waterfowl, but in winter feed almost solely on ptarmigan. If ptarmigan populations are high, gyrfalcons may not leave the Arctic even in winter. Only when ptarmigan reach the low point of their population cycles do gyrfalcons wander south in winter in any numbers.

Gyrfalcons are seldom seen on migration. One or two have been seen over the years at most northern long-running watches, but only Duluth, Minnesota, gets them "regularly"—at a rate of one every other year or so. It is better to search for gyrs in winter. Skagit Flats in Washington may be about the best place, with several present in the area most winters,

and the Canadian plains near Calgary, Alberta, dependably hold a few every winter. In the U.S., Sault Ste. Marie, Michigan, seems to have a gyr every winter, and the Duluth/Superior Harbor area has one from time to time. Each winter there are quite a few in Newfoundland. The only known spring gyrfalcon "migration" is at L'Anse aux Meadows in northern Newfoundland, where up to 30 have been counted heading north.

Because of their rarity and the excitement they generate, hotlines highlight any winter gyr report and can help the prospective seeker. Call hotlines regularly for updates on sightings and specific directions. We have used hotlines to find gyrs near Atlantic City, New

Jersey, a pair in Lancaster County, Pennsylvania, at Sault Ste. Marie in Michigan and at the unlikely destination of the New Haven landfill in Connecticut, where a dark, young male gyr spent an entire winter feasting on starlings and pigeons and was seen by hundreds of birders. Gyrs may occur when you least expect them. Clay found his first one near Cape May on a cold gray January day. Flushed from a remote wetlands roadside post, it spent a few minutes harassing brant, then disappeared to the north, never to be seen again despite a search by dozens of birders. When looking for gyrs, don't be discouraged. They have huge ranges at any season and may visit a given spot only once a day or once every several days. Be patient and fan out through the area, always returning to check the known roost or hunting area.

The gyrfalcon's low, rapid hunting flight brings to mind a giant merlin. Its wing flap is shallow, done mostly with the outer wing (compared to a peregrine). They are deceptively fast, seeming to cover a lot of ground without much flapping. They have long wide tails, and should show translucent or gray flight feathers (unlike peregrines). All plumages should lack the distinct facial mustache mark of a peregrine.

You should be wholly familiar with peregrines before you identify and report a sighting of the much rarer and elusive gyrfalcon.

Gyrfalcons nest on Arctic cliffs in some of the most barren and remote regions on Earth.

How to Spot Hawks & Eagles

Mississippi Kite

Ictinia mississippiensis
Length: 14"
Wingspan: 31"

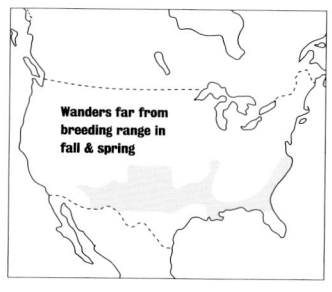

Wanders far from breeding range in fall & spring

The Mississippi kite is a marvelous flier, spending many hours of the day aloft in warm summer skies, hawking insects against billowing white cumulus. Several of our kites, notably the Mississippi and the white-tailed, are remarkably falcon-like in their shape and behavior, although not at all closely related. Mississippi kites are found from Arizona east across the southern Great Plains to northern Florida. Additionally, they nest north up the Mississippi drainage to Kentucky and Indiana and up the East Coast to North Carolina.

In the West, they nest in prairie shelter belts and cottonwoods and in Spanish-moss-draped live oaks along bottomland swamps in the South. Highly migratory, they are gone by early September, spending the winter in South America as far south as Argentina and returning in mid-April.

Several thousand are seen at South Texas hawkwatches each spring and fall, although their broad-front migrations can be hard to intercept. Expert fliers, they are known wanderers, and a few are seen far outside their normal range in spring. In the East, prospecting

Graceful and buoyant fliers, Mississippi kites are quite falcon-like in shape.

birds have extended the breeding range north each spring.

Mississippi kites appear dark at a distance, but the white head of an adult shows well in good light. They are graceful and buoyant fliers, sailing and gliding more than soaring. They can appear quite peregrine-like in flight, but the slow stiff flap of the kite should separate them. A soaring Mississippi kite may look remarkably similar to a broad-winged hawk, but the long splayed tail is a giveaway. Exceptional fliers, they appear more at home in the air than when perched.

White-tailed Kite

Elanus leucurus
Length: 15"
Wingspan: 38½"

The white-tailed kite has pointed, falcon-like wings and is white below and gray-backed with distinctive black shoulder patches. It was formerly called the black-shouldered kite; both names well describe it. The white-tailed kite is widely distributed in South and Central America; in the U.S. it is common only in coastal California and coastal Texas, although it has recently expanded its range into Arizona, Oklahoma, Mississippi and Florida. It is largely nonmigratory, yet a known wanderer. Populations seem partially nomadic, and numbers respond

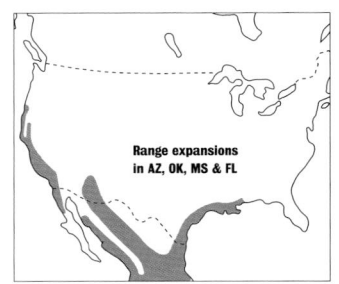

Range expansions
in AZ, OK, MS & FL

Distinctive patches on the white-tailed kite gave it its former name: black-shouldered kite.

to rodent population booms—abundant one year and scarce the next. They form communal nighttime roosts in fall and winter.

Look for the white-tailed kite in open grasslands, fields and agricultural areas, where you can locate it by its distinctive hovering hunting flight as it searches for mammals or insects. It hovers much like an American kestrel, and it both soars and glides with a marked dihedral. Only 20 to 30 are seen at Golden Gate in California every fall and 20 to 30 at South Texas hawkwatches each season. Such numbers mainly indicate dispersal.

For looks at white-tailed kites year-round, try Laguna Atascosa NWR in Texas and environs, where up to 65 have been seen on Christmas Bird Counts. You might find them almost anywhere on the California coast in open areas. Try the Point Reyes National Seashore area and surrounding farmlands.

Swallow-tailed Kite

Elanoides forficatus
Length: 24"
Wingspan: 51"

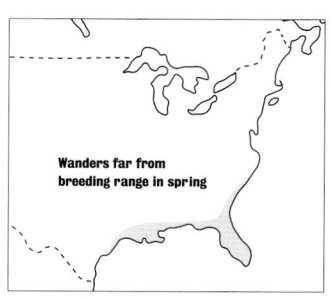

Wanders far from breeding range in spring

The swallow-tailed kite, a graceful master of the southern summer skies, is among the most beautiful of all raptors. At times, it appears to fly in slow motion, either hawking dragonflies or picking anoles (lizards) from treetops. Swallow-tailed kites are very rare nesters in east Texas, becoming more common across

The swallow-tailed kite, with its striking plumage, is one of the most beautiful raptors.

Mississippi, Alabama and North Florida. Strongholds are coastal South Carolina, particularly Francis Marion National Forest, and the Florida Everglades. They arrive in South Florida very early in spring to nest, often as early as late February. They then leave the U.S. by late July, crossing the Florida Straits and island hopping to South America where they spend the winter. Only a few are seen at Texas hawkwatches each season. Known wanderers, several are seen at Cape Hatteras and Cape May each spring. Swallow-tailed kites once had a much larger range in North America, nesting north nearly to the Canadian border.

The swallow-tailed kite ranks near the gyrfalcon as a prized quest for hawk spotters. A sure bet for finding swallow-tails is Everglades National Park in spring. Search the open pine woods around Long Pine Key. Scan low over the treetops for foraging birds from midmorning on. In the Francis Marion National Forest area of South Carolina, try Hampton Plantation State Park or scan midday from Route 17 where it crosses the marshes of the Santee River delta. Birds are present from March through July, and we have seen up to 35 swallow-tails together over the Santee River in June. (Mississippi kites are numerous there too.) The migratory gatherings of swallow-tails near Lake Okeechobee in Florida in late July are legendary; nearly 700 have been seen together near Moore Haven, southwest of Lake Okeechobee. Good numbers have also been tallied over both Alligator Alley (Route 75) and the Tamiami Trail (Route 41) in both spring and late summer.

With its black and white plumage and deeply forked tail, the swallow-tailed kite is unmistakable. When in their range, however, be sure to check all distant white-bellied birds assumed to be osprey, for the swallow-tailed kite is nearly the size of an osprey and shows similarly swept back wings. Their flight is often low and surprisingly slow—the long swallow-like tail feathers act as airfoils, or "flaps," allowing an almost slow-motion flight. The sight of swallow-tails floating over a river of grass on tranquil Florida spring days is raptor spotting at its peak.

Northern Harrier

Circus cyaneus
Length: 18"
Wingspan: 44"

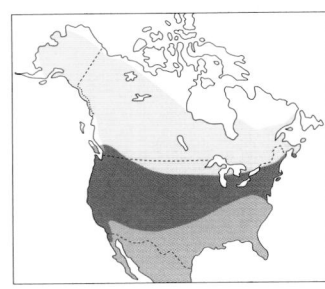

Northern harriers are indeed "hawks of the marshes" as researcher Fran Hammerstrom aptly described them in her delightful book of the same name. The harrier, formerly called the marsh hawk, is a bird of open spaces—marsh, meadow, old fields and grasslands. They only seldom perch in trees, preferring instead perching (and roosting) on the ground or on hummocks, fences, duck blinds or muskrat houses.

Black wing tips and a gray head characterize the soaring adult male northern harrier.

Harriers nest on the ground in marshes and grasslands. Females are warm brown in color.

Although linked to open habitat, they are widespread in North America, abundant on the coasts and less so inland, although a few can be seen each day in almost any open country. Harriers are ground nesters and nest north to northern Alaska and Canada, south to the central U.S., and in winter retire mostly to the lower 48 states. Interestingly, they are on the move throughout the migratory seasons. At Cape May, New Jersey, we see harriers moving south from August through December and north from February through June. Peak flights might come anytime. Cape May sees 3,000-plus in a good fall, with an average of about 1,700. Duluth, Minnesota, records up to 1,200, mostly in September, and Derby Hill in New York records about 750 to 1,000 each

spring. While found daily at most hawk-watches throughout the season, harriers are best viewed in numbers in winter. Our favorite spots are the Gulf Coast coastal marshes, St. Marks NWR in Florida, Sabine NWR in Louisiana, and Anahuac NWR and Aransas NWR in Texas. Southeastern Arizona grasslands are excellent as well. Their communal night roosts are a particularly exciting find— follow flying birds at dusk in hopes of seeing where they are going.

Harriers can be best identified by their distinctive low, quartering, tilting flight. The wings are held in a V, and the white rump patch is clearly visible. Migrants high overhead may look like accipiters or even falcons when gliding. Sexually dimorphic, the female is the warm brown of autumn marshes, the male (often called "the gray ghost") is the color of leaden winter skies and powdery snowfall. Immatures are rusty orange below. Because harriers are polygamous, there are fewer males than females. On the Atlantic Coast, males more often hunt upland fields, while females remain on the vast tidal wetlands. While harriers are mainly linked to mice and vole populations, they are opportunistic—their coursing hunting flights may target anything from red-winged blackbirds to rails.

Osprey

Pandion haliaetus
Length: 23½"
Wingspan: 63"

Often called the "fish hawk," the osprey feeds exclusively on fish and is always found near open water.

The osprey is found throughout the world and is widespread in North America, nesting from northern Alaska east to Labrador and along the coasts to Mexico and the Florida Keys. They are highly migratory, withdrawing to Central and South America in winter, although many winter along the Gulf Coast of Texas and in central and southern Florida. All one-year-old ospreys

Sparse migrant inland

remain on the wintering grounds throughout their first summer and only return north when two years old. They don't breed until their third year. Ospreys build large, bulky stick nests in exposed trees and on artificial platforms and reuse the same nest for many years. Where common, they are colonial nesters, sometimes forming colonies of more than 50 nests. Ospreys are quite vocal during the breeding season, whistling whenever intruders near their nests. They also whistle back and forth to one another during migration when concentrated at places such as the tip of the Cape Charles Peninsula. The "fish hawk," as it was once called, is exclusively a fish eater, catching them by making spectacular feet-first dives into the water, submerging completely.

In fall, ospreys migrate early to mid-season and are seen at hawkwatches from late August to early November. Duluth records about 250, Hawk Mountain about 500. They are mainly coastal migrants; Cape May counts up to 5,000 in a season, with over 800 once seen in a single day. In spring, Whitefish Point counts about 150, Braddock Bay and Derby Hill about 300 to 700. In late winter, the Everglades and the Lake Region of Florida is filled with ospreys. Check the utility poles on the Florida Keys for close looks at nesting ospreys in March and April. We have enjoyed watching ospreys dive for piranha in the tributaries of the Orinoco River in Venezuela in February and have seen their distinctive shapes high over the dry llanos, migrating north. A favorite osprey sighting was on the Jersey marshes in late March, when we watched an early arrival male first spot his returning mate. He quickly left the nest, pumping for altitude and whistling constantly. As he performed his exuberant roller-coaster courtship flight high overhead, she descended to the nest, perched and preened. Home again.

To identify ospreys, always look for the distinctive crooked-wing shape. They soar and glide with the inner portion of the wing raised and outer portion of the wing (the elbow) drooped, creating an M shape when viewed head on. When viewed from below, the inner portion of the wing is thrust far forward and outer portion pulled back, again creating an M. Ospreys often appear more gull-like than hawk-like.

Turkey Vulture

Cathartes aura
Length: 28"
Wingspan: 68"

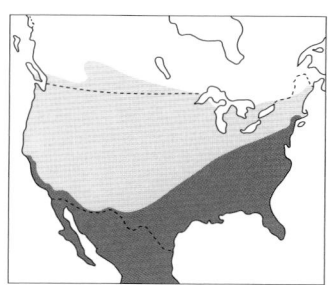

The turkey vulture is found throughout the Western Hemisphere and is the bird of prey most commonly spotted in much of North America. They soar in large groups over open land and roost communally in forests, woodlots and often on man-made structures such as transmission towers and water towers. Turkey vultures are easily identified, even at a great distance, by their large size, dark coloration and wobbling

The turkey vulture's featherless head is well-suited to its carrion-eating existence.

or unsteady flight. They always fly with their wings in a distinct V, whether rising on early morning thermals or buffeted by a rising gale.

Turkey vultures breed north into Canada and are found from the mid-Atlantic states south to Texas in winter, as well as along the California coast. Winter numbers can reach the thousands on the Florida prairies. Recently, 3,600 were found on the Corkscrew Swamp Christmas Bird Count. They are abundant on migration at almost all sites. In the fall, 5,000 can be seen at Golden Gate in California; 3,000 at Cape May. Eight-thousand-plus have been counted at Braddock Bay in New York in the spring. Texas is the turkey vulture capital, where over 30,000 have been seen on spring counts. In the West, the Kern River watch has recorded 27,000 heading south in fall at the southern end of the Sierra Nevada Mountains east of Bakersfield, California, and 10,000 have been counted migrating at a Mojave Desert site in fall. A major migration also occurs at Cape Flattery on the Olympic Peninsula of Washington. An important scavenger, the so-called "turkey buzzard," is an unsung member of our avifauna.

Black Vulture

Coragyps atratus
Length: 25"
Wingspan: 59"

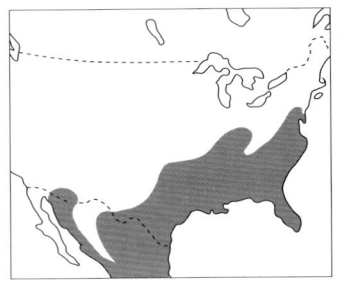

The black vulture has a more southerly distribution than the turkey vulture and is largely nonmigratory. It is resident from New Jersey and Pennsylvania west to Oklahoma and Texas. They are abundant in Central and South America, where we have seen over 2,000 soaring together over the Caracas dump in Venezuela. The black vulture is separated from the turkey vulture by its smaller size, short tail (almost tailless look) and choppy wing beat. The silvery area in the wings is confined to the wingtips and can appear yellowish. Black vultures soar on flat wings or with only a slight dihedral, and form squadrons on high. They are important scavengers and tend to be bolder than turkey vultures.

Black vultures are not hard to spot within their range. They are common on the Delaware Bayshore and in the

Before they can fly, vultures often spread their wings to gather the sun's warmth.

How to Spot Hawks & Eagles

Sometimes maligned, the black vulture is a skilled and graceful soaring bird.

(*Gymnogyps californianus*), is also found in North America but remains on the brink of extinction. By the 1960s, their historic range had dwindled to the coastal range and western foothills of the Sierra Nevada in central and southern California. The few surviving condors were taken into captivity in the 1980s for propagation, and by 1992, offspring were being released into the wild. Further releases are occurring in California's Sierra Madre and the Vermillion Cliffs near the Grand Canyon in Arizona. While a small number of condors once again fly free, they require the strongest protection efforts possible, and only time will tell if we can count on sighting condors soaring high over their ancestral western mountains.

Chesapeake Bay region. Look for them on the Gettysburg battlefield in Pennsylvania, where legend claims they were never found until after the Civil War battle in 1863. Hundreds of black vultures can be seen on Florida cattlelands and on the Texas coast. Try the Kingsville area—the heart of Texas rangeland. A few are seen at hawkwatches each year—a combination of dispersing local birds and wanderers. Black vultures are rapidly expanding their range in the East. In Cape May County, where seeing even one was a red-letter occasion as recently as the 1970s, hundreds can be found today, their roadside clean-ups and effortless soaring a welcome addition.

One other vulture, the **California condor**

Crested Caracara

Caracara plancus
Length: 23"
Wingspan: 50"

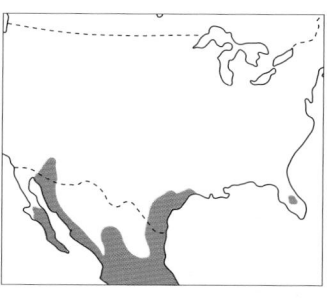

The crested caracara is actually *not* a vulture. It is technically a member of the falcon family but is so unlike falcons in looks and behavior and so like vultures in its scavenging habits and appearance that, for raptor-spotting purposes, it is included here with the other carrion eaters. The caracara is abundant in Central and South America, and its range reaches the U.S. in open prairies, deserts and farmlands of central Florida, southeastern Texas and southern Arizona. It is the national bird of Mexico, the

"Mexican eagle." Primarily a scavenger, caracaras are also pirates, stealing food from vultures and other raptors, and are often, but not always, dominant at a carcass. They do hunt insects, reptiles and amphibians at times. Caracaras are nonmigratory.

To find caracaras, travel back roads around Lake Okeechobee in the Florida prairie region. Drive the loop suggested in the ABA birdfinding guide (see page 131) and scan for birds sitting on the ground in rangeland or perched on fence lines, often right next to the road. Probably the best place in the U.S. to see caracaras is the area around Kingsville, Texas. Here not only do cattle rangelands attract scavengers, but chicken ranches discard carcasses daily. Back roads through this area should yield up to 50 crested caracara in a day. In direct flight, caracaras fly with distinctive rowing wingbeats. They soar seldom, yet well; look for a bird with a shape like a bald eagle, wings like a black vulture and a tail like a golden eagle.

Although related to falcons, the caracara shares the habits and looks of a vulture.

Bald Eagle

Haliaeetus leucocephalus
Length: 32"
Wingspan: 81"

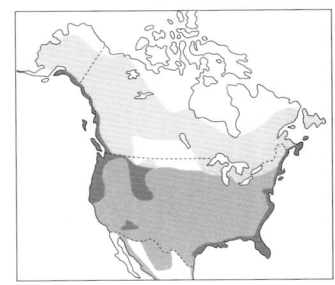

No day afield in search of raptors, no matter how successful or pleasant, is complete without an eagle, and hawkwatchers from South Harpswell in Maine to the Florida Keys, from Cranberry Marsh in Ontario to the Gulf Coast at Baton Rouge, anxiously await the appearance of that dot on the skyline that will slowly, inexorably materialize into an eagle overhead. Happily, with the DDT era behind us, this is now happening with much greater frequency.

The bald eagle is exclusively a North American eagle, nesting from the Aleutian Islands to Newfoundland and south to the Florida Keys and the Baja Peninsula. It is replaced in the Old World by the closely related white-tailed eagle. The bald eagle has a marked affinity for water and is invariably found around lakes, rivers, wetlands and coastlines. Bald eagles are opportunists, but fish usually constitute a majority of their diet. Key places to search for eagles include the Maine coast, the Chesapeake Bay (Blackwater NWR, Maryland, is excellent), the Florida Lake Region and the Everglades (they are hard to miss in the Coot Bay/Flamingo region). In fall, winter and spring, the upper Mississippi and

How to Spot Hawks & Eagles

In the West, salmon runs attract tremendous concentrations of bald eagles.

its tributaries hold many bald eagles. The Klamath Basin in Oregon attracts as many as 1,000 some winters, and the Klamath Basin Bald Eagle Conference, held in mid-February, offers excellent opportunities to see and learn about bald eagles (see page 135). From there north, the British Columbia coast and the inside passage of Alaska host major eagle populations. Coastal Alaska holds many thousands of bald eagles at any season.

While winter is the easiest time to spot bald eagles in numbers, migration also offers the raptor enthusiast many opportunities. Of all the hawkwatches mentioned in this book, only those in South Texas do not see bald eagles annually. Venerable Hawk Mountain in Pennsylvania now records about 80 to 100 bald eagles on migration each fall. Cape May, which bottomed out in 1977 with only 9, now gets 130 to 150 bald eagles, data that illustrates the recovery of this bird from the days of DDT poisoning.

Cape May and Hawk Mountain numbers both reflect dual peaks in this species' migrations in the East. Florida birds migrate north after their early breeding season, often wandering well into Canada. In fall, August and September eagles at hawkwatches are primarily Florida or southern birds returning south for the coming breeding season. October

Immature bald eagles, with variable plumage, look considerably different from their parents.

through December, eagles seen at hawk-watches are northern birds heading south for the winter. In spring, these northern breeders head back in March and April, and the Florida birds subsequently show up in May and June, heading north for the summer. All of this has been learned through banding data.

In spring, Whitefish Point in Michigan gets 30 to 40 bald eagles in March and April and Braddock Bay in New York sees about 130. The champion eagle migration spots are Eagle Valley Nature Center in Wisconsin, where 1,250 have been seen in one fall, and Duluth, Minnesota, where eagle totals are skyrocketing. In the fall of 1994, 4,368 bald eagles were counted from Hawk Ridge in Duluth (along with 133 golden eagles) migrating south into the central U.S., including 743 seen on No-vember 22 alone. As recently as the mid 1980s only an average of about 170 a year were recorded there.

To identify bald eagles, look for large dark birds on flat, plank-like wings. They *never* waiver in the wind as turkey vultures do. Bald eagles have powerful direct flight. Their flap is deep, their wings wide. It takes a bald eagle four years to achieve adult plumage. Adult balds are unmistakable, but immature birds are highly variable. The youngest immatures (first-year birds) are the darkest; three-year-olds can show considerable white in the plumage.

Among immatures, plumages are variable enough that many different individuals can be recognized, an important aspect of winter or migration counting.

How to Spot Hawks & Eagles

Golden Eagle

Aquila chrysaetos
Length: 32"
Wingspan: 80"

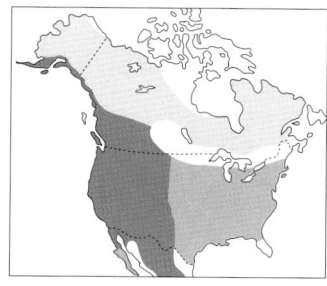

The golden eagle, one of the most magnificent birds of prey, has a worldwide range that includes the mountainous areas of Asia, Europe, the Middle East and North Africa. In North America, they are mostly a bird of western mountains and grasslands, where their favorite prey is jackrabbits, prairie dogs and other ground squirrels. They breed from the north slope of Alaska across Canada and south into Mexico, northern birds withdrawing south in the winter. In the East, they breed on the Gaspé Peninsula and Labrador. Common in the West, they have always been uncommon to rare in the East, except for the large numbers (usually 80 to 90 per year) seen migrating by Hawk Mountain and other lookouts in autumn. The origin of these eastern birds was always debated and only recently learned with the discovery of many pairs of nesting goldens on the eastern shore of Hudson Bay in northern Quebec.

In the East, look for wintering golden eagles in the Chesapeake Bay (try Blackwater NWR) and along the Mullica River, on the coast of New Jersey. Here, try Forsythe (Brigantine) NWR or the end of Leeds Point Road, just north of the refuge, on winter days with a northwest wind. Mornings are best for eagle sightings (both bald and golden) there. Eastern winter goldens select waterfowl as prey, mostly snow geese and black ducks, which they take in flight in spectacular stoops. We once watched a golden kill and feed on a great blue heron. During migration, look for golden eagles in late October and November at northeastern hawkwatches. Hawk Mountain is a staple, but due to the vagaries of geography, both the Franklin Mountain Hawkwatch near Oneonta, New York, and Waggoners Gap in Pennsylvania are the eastern champs, where up to 125 goldens are counted each fall.

Newly founded western hawkwatches clearly show that the golden eagle is really a

White patches at the base of the primary feathers and a dark-tipped white tail distinguish an immature golden.

In North America, golden eagles are mostly birds of the West, preferring mountain areas.

westerner. The Bridger Mountain, Montana, site records up to 1,700 golden eagles each fall, and a new site at Mount Lorette, Alberta, recorded nearly 4,000 golden eagles in 80 days of observation in 1994. Early October is the peak time for goldens here, when up to 200 can be seen in a day. These observation sites on the front range of the Rocky Mountains are recording the flight of goldens leaving the vast Canadian Arctic and Alaskan breeding grounds. In spring, the hawkwatch in the Sandia Mountains in New Mexico records up to 450 birds returning north.

In winter, western goldens are dispersed, but look for them in Colorado and New Mexico grasslands or in any North Texas refuge. Los Padres National Forest north of Los Angeles holds both wintering and nesting golden eagles. The Sulphur Springs Valley in southeast Arizona is particularly popular with both eagles and eagle watchers in winter.

Adult goldens are all dark, with bright gold on the back of the head (the "hackles") showing in good light. In contrast to bald eagles, goldens have a smaller head, neck and bill, and a longer tail. They fly rock steady, with the wings in a marked dihedral. Young goldens show a varying amount of white in the wings and a white tail with a dark tip. To identify immature eagles, note where the white is in the wings. Bald eagles have white at the *base* of the wing (or the "wingpit") on the underwing coverts. Young golden eagles have white near the wing *tips*, on the flight feathers (both the primaries and secondaries), never on the underwing coverts.

How to Spot Hawks & Eagles

Common Black Hawk

Buteogallus anthracinus
Length: 21"
Wingspan: 46"

Zone-tailed Hawk

Buteo albonotatus
Length: 20"
Wingspan: 52"

Gray Hawk

Buteo nitidus
Length: 17"
Wingspan: 35"

Harris' Hawk

Parabuteo unicinctus
Length: 21"
Wingspan: 44"

White-tailed Hawk

Buteo albicaudatus
Length: 20"
Wingspan: 51"

Hook-billed Kite

Chondrohierax uncinatus
Length: 18"
Wingspan: 37"

The striking white tail band of the black hawk sets off its dark plumage.

The desert heat shimmered, and every scan of the binoculars was met with hazy heat waves. To the north, the sagebrush scrub was so bright in the August Arizona sun that it hurt our eyes, even with sunglasses. To the south, the lush green cottonwoods were a relief to look at, and the waters of Aravaipa Creek beckoned. We had found black hawks earlier that day, and one was still in view, but the distant views were unsatisfactory as heat waves distorted the view through our scopes. We had been entertained by several good looks at zone-tailed hawks overhead, but as the heat grew they had soared off to the east, leaving only cloudless blue sky. The black hawk sat. We waited. The radio said it had been 107 degrees F in nearby Tucson at 9:00 A.M., and it was now after noon. By now it seemed at least 125 degrees—about 140 degrees different from six months earlier when we had looked for gyrfalcons in Sault Ste. Marie, Michigan (a not unusual illustration of the extreme conditions that can face raptor enthusiasts).

Louise Zemaitis spotted the bird first as it flapped heavily out of the cottonwood shade and immediately began to soar. "Here it

The rocking flight of a zone-tail is very similar to the flight of a turkey vulture.

comes," she said, "get your camera ready." With buoyant desert lift, the black hawk crested the streamside bluffs and what little wind there was carried the bird right over us. David Sibley and Louise sketched, Clay quickly went through a roll of film, and Pat merely whipered, "Wow!" as the sun gleamed through the bird's beautiful white tail band.

A few species of hawks require specialized searches, as they are found only in very limited areas. The arid southwest has a number of these birds—raptors that barely make it into the U.S. from their normal Central and South American ranges. The **common black hawk** is one such species, uncommon and local during the breeding season only in south central Arizona, western New Mexico and southwest Texas. Look for them in riparian habitats where they prey on crayfish, frogs, fish and reptiles. They are sedentary, spending hours on low perches along cottonwood-lined streams searching for prey. They do soar, however, usually at midday or early afternoon, possibly to cool off. They are a very wide-winged, short-tailed buteo, somewhat like a black vulture in shape. Look for black hawks along Arizona streams north nearly to Flagstaff or in the Davis Mountains of Texas. Check birdfinding guides for specific directions. Never approach a black hawk nest (or that of any raptor) for a "better look."

The **zone-tailed hawk** is found in much the same areas of Arizona as the black hawk, but is more widely distributed in New Mexico and Texas. The zone-tail has a much longer tail than a black hawk. Zone-tails are thought to mimic turkey vultures, allowing them to approach prey undetected. They fly with a marked V in the wings and rock back and

Look for the small gray hawk in Arizona.

How to Spot Hawks & Eagles

forth like a turkey vulture. Found in summer in both dry riparian habitat and mountain live oak or pinyon pine forests and canyons, most migrate south in winter. Zone-tails should be easily seen, for example, by watching the summer skies over The Nature Conservancy's Patagonia-Sonoita Creek Preserve at Patagonia, Arizona. Anywhere in the Santa Rita Mountains, or much of Coronado National Forest, offers a good chance of spotting them. Remember to scan turkey vulture flocks for this look-alike. To illustrate how much a zone-tailed hawk can look like a turkey vulture, we once watched two young zone-tails in their nest give food-begging calls to every turkey vulture that flew over.

The **gray hawk** is another southwestern specialty. This small, active buteo has a rapid and accipiter-like flight. Its short wings and long tail are used to maneuver rapidly in its pursuit of lizards, mammals and small birds. Look for the gray hawk in its limited North American range in riparian areas of southeast Arizona. The Santa Cruz River and Sonoita Creek area are good; the San Pedro River is best, where probably 40 percent of the U.S. population is found. Hike trails along the river in the San Pedro Riparian National Conservation Area, east of Sierra Vista, managed by the Federal Bureau of Land Management. Scan cottonwoods, streamside perches and the sky. Black hawks are sometimes found here too. In Texas, a few individuals or pairs of gray hawks can be found in the Rio Grande Valley. Check all buteos seen at Santa Ana NWR.

Santa Ana NWR in Texas is also an excellent place to spot **Harris' hawks**, with a number of pairs resident both there and at nearby Bentsen-Rio Grande Valley State Park. The Harris' hawk is a dark, beautiful, buteo-like hawk of dry scrub and brush country of the Southwest. Harris' hawks hunt cooperatively, with an entire family group joining to chase

Harris' hawks hunt cooperatively, seeking ground squirrels, gophers and rabbits.

ground squirrels, gophers and rabbits. Harris' hawks are fairly common, conspicuous and easily spotted within their range, often perching on roadside utility poles. Try the Rio Grande Valley of Texas at any season (they are nonmigratory) or Laguna Atascosa NWR. They are common in cattle grazing lands near

The white-tailed hawk, *top*, and the hook-billed kite, *bottom*, are tropical species found in the U.S. only in South Texas.

Kingsville, Texas. In Arizona, try mesquite and thorny brushlands of the Sonoran Desert region around Tucson. Consult birdfinding guides for particulars.

The handsome **white-tailed hawk** is confined in the U.S. to the coastal region of Texas. Nonmigratory, it can be found at any season. White-tailed hawks are highly active, hunt-

ing lizards, snakes, birds and mammals while on the wing. They kite and hover high overhead and make long dives into the brush, often congregating over prairie fires or brush fires for opportunistic feeding. White-tails are fairly common in coastal prairie and chaparral and agricultural areas from Galveston to Brownsville. Scan for them at Aransas NWR and Laguna Atascosa NWR. The Kingsville region again is good. Check near cattle and chicken ranches. Adults will look similar to Swainson's hawks from below, but have a white tail with a dark terminal band. Immatures are very dark below.

The **hook-billed kite** is primarily a resident of the tropics, only making it into the U.S. in the lower Rio Grande Valley of Texas. Here, in the mesquite woodlands from Falcon Dam east to Santa Ana NWR, a few pairs are resident but hard to spot. They are fairly sedentary and eat tree snails deep within the scrub forest. You can sometimes spot hook-billed kites while walking refuge trails, but your best bet is to find them soaring above the canopy. Watch from the dikes along the boundaries of Bentsen-Rio Grande Valley State Park. At Santa Ana NWR, watch from the dikes or hike around Pintail Lake, scanning the skies to the south toward the Rio Grande River. Most days, hook-billed kites will soar in mid to late morning, particularly in the spring when they perform dramatic courtship flights daily. Hook-billed kites have three distinct plumages. Males are dark gray, females rufous below, and young birds are lighter brown. They are distinctive in flight with a long broad tail, paddle-shaped wings, deep slow wingbeats and bowed wings while gliding or soaring.

How to Spot Hawks & Eagles

Short-tailed Hawk
Buteo brachyurus
Length: 16"
Wingspan: 37"

Snail Kite
Rostrhamus sociabilis
Length: 17½"
Wingspan: 42½"

On hot humid spring days in South Florida, thermals are generous and abundant. Boiling cumulus fills the sky over the Everglades. In these conditions, **short-tailed hawks** excel. Rare for a buteo, the short-tailed hawk is exclusively a bird hunter, and in these dramatic Florida skies, we watched a pair make repeated spectacular stoops into the forest canopy, rising again on the building thermals as if on an elevator. Just two or three minutes later, they were kiting again, specks against the clouds, ready to repeat the stoop. We have watched this exciting behavior in short-tailed hawks in Florida, Mexico and Venezuela—a treat for the raptor spotter.

This tropical species reaches the U.S. only in Florida, where it is found in small numbers in mixed woodlands, savannahs and prairie. They are partially migratory, withdrawing from the Florida Peninsula south to the Everglades and Keys in winter. Then they are found around cypress and mangrove wetlands. They are most concentrated in December and January and therefore most easily found then. Look anywhere in Everglades National Park, where up to ten have been found on the Christmas Bird Count. We have found the Long Pine Key area best, particularly the road to Royal Palm Hammock. We have also found them in the Florida Keys, on Big Pine Key at Key Deer NWR. In breeding season, try Fisheating Creek Wildlife Management Area west of Palmdale and Big Cypress National Preserve.

The Everglades and Florida Keys are the best places in the U.S. where a short-tailed hawk might be seen.

Snail kites feast exclusively on aquatic snails plucked from marshes and lake margins.

Short-tailed hawks occur in both dark and light forms. In Florida, only about 20 percent of the population is light form. Dark-form birds have silvery flight feathers not unlike a dark rough-legged hawk. Light-form short-tails have dark flight feathers like Swainson's hawks, which sometimes share South Florida skies in winter. There may be some exchange between Florida short-tails and those from farther south (Cuba or South America) as evidenced by a recent record at the Dry Tortugas. There are also a few very recent sight records from south Texas and southern Arizona, but this species should not be expected there.

Another tropical species that is only found in the U.S. in South Florida is the **snail kite**, once parochially called the "Everglades kite." Found from Argentina north to Mexico, and in Cuba, they feed almost exclusively on aquatic snails of the genus *Pomacea*, known as apple snails. They are social, often found in loose flocks as they forage for snails, which they pluck from below the water surface of sloughs, marshes and lake edges. They nest and roost colonially as well.

Florida snail kite populations have fluctuated greatly in this century. They were victims of drought and of the loss of water in the Everglades and are now benefitting from Everglades restoration efforts. The Florida population has been as low as 65, but is currently thought to be over 500 individuals. It is listed as an endangered species. The pre-

How to Spot Hawks & Eagles

sent range of the snail kite in Florida extends from the headwaters of the St. Johns River, through the Kissimmee basin, south through Lake Okeechobee to the northern part of Everglades National Park. Look for snail kites at Shark Valley in Everglades National Park (off of Route 41, the Tamiami Trail). A good spot over the years has been the section of the Tamiami Trail that passes through the Miccosukee Reservation, particularly near the Miccosukee Restaurant. Scan wet areas from roadside pull-offs.

Snail kites are sometimes seen at Loxahatchee NWR and can be spotted in Lake Okeechobee by boat. In recent years, some of the lakes north of Okeechobee have attracted snail kites, including Lake Istokpoga. Snail kites are itinerant, actually nomadic, in response to water levels and related snail abundance. Consult the latest edition of bird-finding guides when planning a trip, and call hotlines when in the area.

When looking for snail kites, scan over sawgrass, cattail marshes and wet prairies. Search for a bird patrolling slowly over the marshes not unlike a harrier. They are round-winged kites and can look quite buteo-like, soaring high above the marshes. Males are slate gray, females are brown above and streaked below. Both have white at the base of the tail (like harriers) but have a distinctive bowed or cupped wing appearance whether flapping, gliding or soaring over their flooded Florida wetland haunts.

Swooping down onto Everglade waters at sunset, a bald eagle zeroes in on a fish.

Swainson's hawk.

Further Information

HAWK & EAGLE IDENTIFICATION

Campbell, R. Wayne, ed. *Know Your Birds of Prey: Vultures to Falcons*. Axia CD ROM for PC (requires Windows 3.1). 1995. Multimedia approach to hawk identification for all diurnal raptors of North America. Includes multiple photos, sketches, and full-motion video clips of perched and flying birds, field marks, shape, call, habitat and range maps.

Clark, William S. and Brian Wheeler. *Hawks* (Peterson Field Guide Series). Houghton Mifflin Company: Boston, 1987. A must-have book for the raptor enthusiast. Besides being a field guide, it is an excellent reference book. The best for raptor plumage.

Connor, Jack. *The Complete Birder*. Houghton Mifflin: Boston, 1988. One chapter on hawks, their identification, and hawkwatching spots. Packed with valuable information about one of North America's most popular pastimes.

Dunne, Pete, Debbie Keller, and Rene Kochenberger. *Hawk Watch, A Guide for Beginners*. Cape May Bird Observatory/New Jersey Audubon Society: Cape May Point, New Jersey, 1984. Comprehensive beginners' guide to hawk identification and hawkwatching.

Dunne, Pete, David Sibley, and Clay Sutton. *Hawks in Flight, The Flight Identification of North American Migrant Raptors*. Houghton Mifflin Company: Boston, 1988. A combination field guide and reference on the holistic approach to hawk identification: using shape, silhouette, flight style and behavior.

Kaufman, Kenn. *Advanced Birding* (Peterson Field Guide Series). Houghton Mifflin Company: Boston, 1990. One chapter on the tough identification of accipiters (sharp-shinned, Cooper's hawk and northern goshawk). Designed for the intermediate to advanced birder.

Porter, R.F., Ian Willis, Steen Christensen, and Bent Pors Nielsen. *Flight Identification of European Raptors*. T. & A.D. Poyser Limited: England, 1981. The European equivalent of, and model for, *Hawks In Flight*, by Dunne, Sibley, and Sutton. A must for the Old World traveler.

Wheeler, Brian K. and William S. Clark. *A Photographic Guide to North American Raptors*. Academic Press Limited: London, 1995. A companion identification guide to *Hawks*. The best photographs of raptors ever assembled. One of our favorites.

MIGRATION

Brett, James J. *The Mountain & the Migration, a Guide to Hawk Mountain.* Hawk Mountain Sanctuary Association: Kempton, Pennsylvania, 1986. The best guide to the place it all began, and a good primer on migration.

Broun, Maurice. *Hawks Aloft, the Story of Hawk Mountain.* Kutztown Publishing Company: Kutztown, Pennsylvania, 1949. A conservation classic, one we have read again and again.

Chartier, Allen and Dave Stimac. *Hawks of Holiday Beach, A Guide to Their Identification, Occurrence, and Habits at Holiday Beach Conservation Area, Ontario, Canada.* Holiday Beach Migration Observatory: Ann Arbor, Michigan, 1993. A must for anyone planning to visit Holiday Beach, but very useful for all hawkwatchers.

Connor, Jack. *Season at the Point, The Birds and Birders of Cape May.* Atlantic Monthly Press: New York, 1991. A book about the essence of the migration at Cape May as it appears to the birders and banders who frequent the Point.

Hawk Migration Studies. Biannual journal of the Hawk Migration Association of North America (HMANA). Managing Editor: Jeffrey Dodge, c/o Braddock Bay Raptor Research, 432 Manitou Beach Road, Hilton, New York 14468. Includes special features, continental summaries and regional reports of spring and fall hawkwatches across Canada, the United States and Mexico. Any serious hawkwatcher needs to join HMANA. The journal gives the results of all hawkwatches throughout the country, not just the major ones.

Heintzelman, Donald S. *Autumn Hawk Flights, the Migrations in Eastern North America.* Rutgers University Press: New Brunswick, New Jersey, 1975. One of the classics. The first book to cover hawk migration and hawkwatching in depth.

Heintzelman, Donald S. *A Guide to Hawk Watching in North America.* Pennsylvania State University: University Park, Pennsylvania, 1979. A companion guide to the previous book. Good photographs and site guides to hawkwatches and raptor viewing areas.

Kerlinger, Paul. *Flight Strategies of Migrating Hawks.* University of Chicago Press: Chicago, 1989. A scholarly treatise and a classic on the dynamics of raptor migration. A must have for the serious student.

Kerlinger, Paul. *How Birds Migrate.* Stackpole Books: Mechanicsburg, Pennsylvania, 1995. Excellent layman's version of the above book. Raptors receive good coverage.

BEHAVIOR

Bent, Arthur Cleveland. *Life Histories of N. American Birds of Prey, Vol. 1 and 2.* Dover Publications, Inc.: New York, 1961. Based on firsthand experiences from researchers all over North America who corresponded with Bent in the 1800s and early 1900s. Though dated, it holds the secret to many questions about raptors because the early researchers were highly interested in natural history and behavior. Excellent educational photographs of nest sites.

Craighead, John J. & Frank C. *Hawks, Owls and Wildlife.* Dover Publications, Inc.: New York, 1969. A classic study of predator-prey ecology.

Dunne, Pete. *The Wind Masters, The Lives of North American Birds of Prey.* Houghton Mifflin Company: Boston, 1995. A classic in the making. Each chapter covers a different aspect of raptor ecology. Penetrating and provocative prose. Beautifully illustrated by David Sibley.

Ehrlich, Paul, David Dobkin, and Darryl Wheye. *The Birder's Handbook*, A Field Guide to the Natural History of North American Birds. Simon & Schuster, Inc.: New York, 1988. Like having a naturalist along with you sharing a steady stream of fascinating and little-known facts. The essays relating to hawks and eagles are superb, such as: "Soaring," "How Fast and How High Do Birds Fly?" "DDT and Birds," "Conservation of Raptors," "Piracy," "Raptor Hunting," "Size and Sex in Raptors," "Hawk-Eyed," "Wing Shapes and Flight," "Adaptations For Flight," "How Long Can Birds Live?" and "Hovering Flight."

SPECIES ACCOUNTS

Baker, J.A. *The Peregrine*. Harper & Row, Publishers: New York, 1967. Our all-time favorite raptor book. Evocative and literary account of one man's story of watching peregrines through the seasons.

Hamerstrom, Frances. *Harrier, Hawk of the Marshes*. Smithsonian Institution Press: Washington, D.C., 1986. Flowing accounts of a researcher's life with harriers.

Poole, Alan F. *Ospreys, A Natural and Unnatural History*. Cambridge University Press: Cambridge, England, 1989. In-depth, scientific yet readable. The last word on ospreys.

GENERAL RAPTOR WORKS

Johnsgard, Paul A. *Hawks, Eagles, & Falcons of North America*. Smithsonian Institution Press: Washington, D.C., 1990. A comprehensive study; detailed accounts of the lives of North American raptors. Helpful range maps.

Journal of Raptor Research. Quarterly publication of the Raptor Research Foundation, Inc., 14377 117th Street South, Hastings, Minnesota 55033. Scientific papers on all aspects of raptor biology.

Palmer, Ralph S., ed. *Handbook of North American Birds*. Vol. 4 and 5: Diurnal Raptors. Yale University Press: New Haven, Connecticut, 1988. The most in-depth work available on all North American species. 900 pages on raptors.

Newton, Ian, ed. *Birds of Prey*. Facts On File: New York, 1990. A very well-done coffee-table approach. Particularly good section on conservation.

Newton, Ian. *Population Ecology of Raptors*. Buteo Books: Vermillion, South Dakota, 1979. Another classic; for the scientist and enthusiastic layman.

Snyder, Noel and Helen. *Birds of Prey, Natural History and Conservation of North American Raptors*. Voyageur Press: Stillwater, Minnesota, 1991. One of our favorites. A good conservation primer and plea.

Sutton, Clay and Richard K. Walton. *North American Birds of Prey (National Audubon Society Pocket Guide)*. Chanticleer Press/Alfred A. Knopf: New York, 1994. A starter's guide to raptors and raptor identification.

Zoobooks. *Birds of Prey*. Wildlife Education, Ltd., 930 West Washington Street, San Diego, California 92103, 1980. Written for children; includes information about hawks, eagles and owls. Beautifully illustrated, making concepts easy to understand. Good learning tool for children.

Zoobooks. *Eagles*. Wildlife Education, Ltd., 930 West Washington Street, San Diego, California 92103, 1983. Same as above but focused on eagles.

TRAVEL

ABA/Lane Birdfinding Guides. *A Birder's Guide to . . . .* (Southeast Arizona, Arkansas, Eastern Massachusetts, Churchill, Texas Coast, Wyoming, Rio Grande Valley of Texas,

Southern California, Colorado, Florida, New Hampshire) and *Birdfinder: A Birder's Guide to Planning North American Trips.* ABA/Lane Series. These books allow for self-guided visits to a region's most productive and interesting birding areas and are regularly updated with new directions, maps and details. These books are available in most nature center bookstores, or write to the ABA Sales address below.

American Birding Association. *Birdfinding in Forty National Forests and Grasslands* (Supplement to *Birding*, Vol. XXVI: No. 2). April 1994. A definitive guide to selected public open-space areas throughout the country. Directions and maps, as well as addresses and phone numbers for more information.

American Birding Association Sales (ABA), P.O. Box 6599, Colorado Springs, Colorado 80934. (800-634-7736).

1. Newsletter, *Winging It*, published monthly, normally includes a birder's guide to a little-known hotspot in North America, details on good birds from the previous month's hotlines around North America, an up-to-date list of all "Rare Bird Alert" (Birding Hotline) phone numbers in North America, and a variety of other articles.

2. *ABA Sales Annotated Catalog and Price List* offers, by mail-order, a complete list of regional birding guides (arranged by state for the U. S., by province for Canada, and by country for the rest of the world), sound recordings, optics and accessories.

3. *Birding*, published bimonthly, often includes thorough book reviews of bird books and sound recordings. Also the "Tools of the Trade" article is informative.

Buff, Sheila. *The Birder's Sourcebook, a Compendium of Essential Birding Information.* Lyons & Burford, Publishers: New York, 1994. Excellent and up-to-date source of birding products, places and organizations.

National Audubon Society. *Field Notes* (formerly *American Birds*), 700 Broadway, NY, NY 10003 (212-979-3000). Five publications each year (Spring, Summer, Fall, Winter and Christmas Bird Count Issue) annotating seasonal bird records around the country. The Christmas Bird Count issue includes the results of over 1,500 counts across the country. High counts for each species presented, making it a quick way to learn where the best areas are to spot each given species.

Riley, Laura and William. *Guide to the National Wildlife Refuges, How to Get There, What to See and Do.* Doubleday: Garden City, New York, 1979.

LEARNING HAWK & EAGLE CALLS

A Field Guide to Bird Songs of Eastern & Central North America (Peterson Field Guide Series). Roger T. Peterson, ed., 1983. Two cassettes or one compact disc.

A Field Guide to Western Bird Songs. Cornell Laboratory, 1992. Three cassettes or two compact discs with booklet (keyed to Peterson's revised *Field Guide to Western Birds*).

Guide to Bird Sounds. Cornell Laboratory, 1985. Two cassettes keyed to National Geographic Society's *Field Guide to the Birds of North America.*

LEARN FROM THE EXPERTS

Braddock Bay Raptor Research, 432 Manitou Beach Road, Hilton, NY 14468. Phone: 716-392-5685. Newsletter, *The Raptor Researcher*, is published twice each year. Spring migration hotspot on southern shore of Lake Ontario. Official hawk count conducted from hawk-watch platform in Braddock Bay State Park;

manned by education interns during the peak of the season. Since 1989, has hosted the annual "Bird of Prey Week" during the last week of April at the peak of the broad-winged hawk migration; this week-long family event includes birds of prey arts, crafts and games, a six-foot mascot ("The Incredible Hawk"), slide presentations, hawk identification classes, hawkwatching and hawk banding demonstrations.

From mid-March through mid-May "Hawk Banding Demonstrations" are offered each Saturday and Sunday, and "Hawk Walks" (slide presentation followed by hawk identification on the hawkwatch platform) are offered each Saturday. Winter raptor field trips to Point Peninsula can be scheduled.

Cape May Bird Observatory, New Jersey Audubon Society, P.O. Box 3, 707 E. Lake Drive, Cape May Point, NJ 08212. Phone: 609-884-2736. Fax: 609-884-6052. Bird Hotline: 609-884-2626. Newsletter, *Peregrine Observer*, is published twice each year. Fall migration hotspot at tip of first major peninsula on East Coast; official hawk count conducted from hawkwatch platform at tip of peninsula in Cape May Point State Park where Delaware Bay and Atlantic Ocean meet. Hawkwatch manned by education interns during the peak of the season. Hawk identification workshops offered every Friday and Saturday in September and October. Daily bird walks. Week-long birding workshop with a focus on raptors include "The Raptor Migration Peak" each October and "Hawks, Owls, and Waterfowl" each January. Field trips in mid-February for "Winter Raptors of the Delaware Bayshore" offer good looks at bald eagles, rough-legged hawks and many other raptors. Since 1947, New Jersey Audubon Society has hosted the "Cape May Autumn Weekend," held at the peak of the hawk migration in late September/early October. This three-day event includes hawk-

watching, identification workshops for raptors and other birds, as well as numerous natural history workshops, programs and walks.

Golden Gate Raptor Observatory, Building 201, Fort Mason, San Francisco, CA 94123. Phone: 415-331-0730. Newsletter, *The Pacific Raptor Report*. Official hawkwatch conducted from atop Hawk Hill in the Marin Headlands, part of the Golden Gate National Recreation Area. In September and October, "Hawk Talks" and "Hawk Banding Demonstrations" offered on weekends (weather permitting) atop Hawk Hill.

Hawk Mountain Sanctuary Association, RR 2, Box 191, Kempton, PA 19529-9449. Phone: 610-756-6961. Fax: 610-756-4468. *Hawk Mountain News* is published twice each year (includes fall hawkwatch report and daily totals). Fall migration hotspot on Kittatinny Ridge. Official hawkwatch conducted from North Lookout, a rocky promontory. Hawkwatch manned by education interns during the peak of the season. "Raptors Alive," a close-up look and learning session with two live birds of prey, is offered every Saturday and Sunday in May and June. Raptor identification program offered every Saturday and Sunday, September through November.

Field courses for college credit or just for fun include "Dynamics of Raptor Migration," "Nesting Biology of Raptors," and "Winter Ecology of Raptors." "Veracruz Hawkwatch" trip each fall (late September through early October) to Mexico, where 3.3 million raptors were recorded during the fall of 1994.

Hawk Ridge Research Station, managed by Duluth Audubon Society, c/o Biology Department, University of Minnesota, Duluth, MN 55812. *Hawk Ridge Annual Report* is published annually and covers fall hawkwatch report and daily totals, hawk and owl banding station report and monthly totals, the passerine banding report and totals, and news of upcoming birding weekends and events. Fall migration hotspot on southwest shore of Lake Superior. At the peak of the fall hawk migration, the Minnesota Ornithologist's Union and Hawk Ridge Nature Reserve co-sponsor several annual Minnesota Birding Weekends focusing on raptors and featuring hawkwatching, identification, hawk and owl banding and many other natural history events ("September Hawk Weekend" is held in mid-September, "October Duluth Weekend" is held in mid-October, and a one-day "Hawk Ridge Day" is offered in late September or early October.) Other weekend trips for spring and winter raptor explorations are also cosponsored by these two groups. For more information contact Kim Eckert at Hawk Ridge Nature Reserve, c/o Biology Dept., U.M.D., Duluth, MN 55812, or call 218-525-6930.

HawkWatch International, P.O. Box 660, 555 E. South Temple, Salt Lake City, UT 84110-0660. Headquarters Phone (in Utah): 800-726-4295; Fax: 801-524-8520. New Mexico Office Phone: 505-255-7622. Quarterly newsletter, *Raptor Watch*, covers fall and spring hawkwatch totals at the various sites, hawk banding station reports, banding recovery reports, and features on specific raptors. Oversees and networks ten raptor migration monitoring sites in the West: seven in the fall (Goshute Mountains in Nevada, Wellsville Mountains in Utah, Manzano Mountains in New Mexico, Grand Canyon's Lipan Point in Arizona, Bridger Mountains in Montana, Bonney Butte in Oregon, and Wenatchee in Washington) and three in the spring (Sandia Mountains in New Mexico, Rogers Pass in Montana, and Cape Flattery in Washington). Visitors are welcome at all sites. Contact HawkWatch International for specific information on access, peak dates, best winds for flights, numbers of raptors seen in a season, etc. HawkWatch International offers a five-week raptor identification course, raptor iden-

tification seminars, and spontaneous banding demonstrations during the peak of the season at hawkwatches where banding also occurs. "Bridger Eagle Day" is held the first two weekends in October, when up to 200 golden eagles a day may migrate through; contact Bridger Ranger District of Gallatin National Forest in Bozeman, Montana, at 406-587-6920 for details.

Southeastern Arizona Bird Observatory, P.O. Box 5521, Bisbee, AZ 85603-5521. Phone: 520-432-1388. Winter raptor tours and workshops in the Sulphur Springs Valley, famous for ferruginous hawks, prairie falcons and eagles. Summer tours of the San Pedro River, stronghold for nesting gray hawks.

Whitefish Point Bird Observatory, HC 48, Box 115, Paradise, MI 49768. Phone: 906-492-3596. Newsletter, *The Migrant*, highlights research projects and education opportunities. Spring migration hotspot on southeast shore of Lake Superior. Official hawk count conducted from hawkwatch platform overlooking Lake Superior. "Morning Bird Walks" every Saturday and Sunday (mid-April through May) visit the hawkwatch platform and help participants improve their birding skills. "Morning Bird-Banding Talks," offered the same days, offer close-up views of hawks and land birds and share discoveries being made by the banding project. Observatory-sponsored winter tours, based in Sault Ste. Marie area, are offered from early January to early March focusing on northern specialities, including gyrfalcons, bald eagles, hawk owls and snowy owls.

RAPTOR FESTIVALS
(other than those offered by the groups above)

Alaska Bald Eagle Festival, P.O. Box 1449, Haines, AK 99827. Phone: 907-766-2202. Festival held in mid-November to witness the gathering of up to 4,000 bald eagles attracted to salmon in the Chilkat River Valley.

Eaglefest, P.O. Box 695, Emory, TX 75440. Phone: 903-473-2377. Annual festival in mid-January celebrating the "Eagle Capital of Texas."

Eagles Weekend, Lake Barkley State Resort Park, Box 790, Cadiz, KY 42211. Phone: 502-924-1131. Since 1972, this annual family weekend has been held in mid-February to witness the winter gathering of eagles at the 170,000-acre Land Between the Lakes National Recreation Area. Includes eagle viewing van and bus trips, boat tours, a workshop on photographing raptors, a live raptor demonstration and evening programs.

Eagle Watch, Winona Convention and Visitor Bureau, P.O. Box 870, Winona, MN 55987-0870. Phone: 800-657-4972 or 507-452-2272. Annual event held in early March; features field trips to prime eagle watching areas along the Mississippi River and Lake Pepin, and presentations about eagle ecology.

Festival of Hawks, Essex Region Conservation Authority, 360 W. Fairview Avenue, Essex, Ontario N8M 1Y6. Phone: 519-766-5209. Held on September weekends at Holiday Beach Conservation Area during the peak of the broad-winged hawk migration, when up to 1,000 hawks per day can be seen. Features hawk banding demonstrations, guest speakers and hawk identification workshops.

Kern Valley Vulture Festival, Kern River Preserve, P.O. Box 1662, Weldon, CA 93283. Phone: 619-378-2531. Festival held in late September to witness the largest-known vulture migration north of Mexico. Also seen are migrating red-tails, Swainson's hawks, ospreys, Cooper's hawks, golden eagles and prairie falcons.

Klamath Basin Bald Eagle Conference, Oregon Department of Fish and Wildlife, 1850 Miller Island Road West, Klamath Falls, OR 97603. Phone: 503-883-5732. Since 1980, this annual conference has been held in mid-February to witness the largest concentration of bald eagles in the lower 48 states; the Klamath Basin area attracts as many as 1,000 bald eagles each winter. Conference includes raptor identification workshops and other indoor programs, an art show and photography competition, guided tours of Lower Klamath NWR and eagle roost watches at Bear Valley NWR, where hundreds of bald eagles congregate.

Quad Cities Bald Eagle Days, Quad City Conservation Alliance, 2621 Fourth Avenue, Rock Island, IL 61201. Phone: 309-788-5912. Festival in late January to witness the bald eagles that winter along the Mississippi River; programs include field trips, eagle ecology, conservation programs and a wildlife art show.

Upper Skagit Bald Eagle Festival, P.O. Box 571, Concrete, WA 98237. Phone: 360-853-7009. Festival in early February featuring one of the largest wintering concentrations of bald eagles in the lower 48 states; eagle tours, roadside viewing sites and raft trips.

Wings Over Willcox, Willcox Chamber of Commerce, 1500 North Circle I Road, Willcox, AZ 85643. Phone: 800-200-2272. Festival held third weekend in January to witness wintering sandhill cranes and raptors in the Sulphur Springs Valley.

Winter Wings Festival, Lake Chicot State Park, 2542 Highway 257, Lake Village, AR 71653. Phone: 501-265-5480. Festival in early February to witness wintering bald eagles and waterfowl along an oxbow of the Mississippi River.

Index

Photography and Illustration Credits

PATRICIA & CLAY SUTTON
14–15, 18, 22, 24, 26 bottom left, 28, 29, 31, 33, 35, 39, 40, 44, 47, 48, 52, 56, 60, 65, 67, 70, 71, 77, 86 top, 93, 97, 102

BRIAN K. WHEELER
26 top left & right & bottom right, 37, 61, 81, 88, 89, 91, 104, 110, 115, 119, 124 bottom, 125

WENDY SHATTIL & BOB ROZINSKI
59, 62, 73, 105, 114, 117, 118

JOHN SHAW
16, 58, 83, 101, 112, 113, 128

ANTHONY MERCIECA
46, 53, 107, 108, 111, 123

TOM & PAT LEESON
42, 45, 106, 120, 127

W. S. CLARK
85, 121, 122, 124 top

RON AUSTING
21, 55, 86 bottom, 95

NED HARRIS
23, 76, 82, 109, 126

KEVIN T. KARLSON
51, 100, 116

TOM VEZO
69, 72, 96

ART WOLFE
78–79, 103

MASLOWSKI PHOTO
49, 84

BRYAN MUNN
17

SHERM SPOELSTRA
54

GREG DODGE
74

KEITH A. SZAFRANSKI
90

F. A. CLELAND
92

DUDLEY EDMONDSON
98

RANGE MAPS
Created by Eugenie Seidenberg Delaney

About the Authors

CLAY SUTTON is a wildlife biologist, naturalist and bird-tour leader. He is the coauthor of *Hawks in Flight* with Pete Dunne and Dave Sibley, the coauthor of *North American Birds of Prey (National Audubon Society Pocket Guide)* with Richard Walton, and coauthor with his wife, Patricia, of *How To Spot An Owl*.

Patricia Taylor Sutton is the Teacher Naturalist at New Jersey Audubon Society's Cape May Bird Observatory. Formerly, she was Senior Naturalist at Cape May Point State Park. In these two positions, she has taught thousands about the wonders of hawks, eagles and owls. She is the author of New Jersey Audubon Society's publication, *Backyard Habitat For Birds, a Guide for Landowners and Communities in New Jersey.*

The Suttons, appropriately, live near Cape May, New Jersey, a location that has been called the Raptor Capital of North America in reference to the spectacular autumn hawk migration there.

101 WAYS TO PROMOTE YOUR WEB SITE

Filled with Proven Internet Marketing Tips, Tools, Techniques, and Resources to Increase Your Web Site Traffic

Other Titles of Interest From Maximum Press

Business-to-Business Internet Marketing: Silverstein, 1-885068-35-2

Marketing on the Internet, Third Edition: Zimmerman, Mathiesen, 1-885068-26-3

Exploring IBM's Bold Internet Strategy: Hoskins, Lupiano, 1-885068-23-9

Exploring IBM Technology & Products, Second Edition: edited by Hoskins, 1-885068-31-X

Building Intranets With Lotus Notes & Domino 5.0, Second Edition: Steve Krantz, 1-885068-24-7

Exploring IBM Personal Computers, 10th Edition: Hoskins, Wilson, 1-885068-25-5

Exploring IBM AS/400 Computers, Ninth Edition: Hoskins, Dimmick, 1-885068-34-4

Exploring IBM RS/6000 Computers, Ninth Edition: Hoskins, Davies, 1-885068-27-1

Exploring IBM's New Age Mainframes, Sixth Edition: Hoskins, Fletcher, 1-885068-30-1

For more information, visit our World Wide Web site at:
http://www.maxpress.com
or e-mail us at *moreinfo@maxpress.com*

101 WAYS TO PROMOTE YOUR WEB SITE

Filled with Proven Internet Marketing Tips, Tools, Techniques, and Resources to Increase Your Web Site Traffic

Susan Sweeney

MAXIMUM PRESS
605 Silverthorn Road
Gulf Breeze, FL 32561
(850) 934-0819
www.maxpress.com

8-6-99

Publisher: Jim Hoskins

Manager of Finance/Administration: Donna Tryon

Production Manager: ReNae Grant

Cover Design: Lauren Smith Designs

Compositor: PageCrafters Inc.

Copyeditor: Janis Paris

Proofreader: Deborah Miller

Indexer: Susan Olason

Printer: Malloy Lithographing

This publication is designed to provide accurate and authoritative information in regard to the subject matter covered. It is sold with the understanding that the publisher is not engaged in rendering professional services. If legal, accounting, medical, psychological, or any other expert assistance is required, the services of a competent professional person should be sought. ADAPTED FROM A DECLARATION OF PRINCIPLES OF A JOINT COMMITTEE OF THE AMERICAN BAR ASSOCIATION AND PUBLISHERS.

Library of Congress Cataloging-in-Publication Data

Sweeney, Susan, 1956-

 101 ways to promote your website / Susan Sweeney.

 p. cm.

 ISBN 1-885068-37-9 (alk. paper)

 1. Internet marketing. 2. Web sites--Marketing. I. Title. II. Title: One hundred one ways to promote your website III. Title: One hundred and one ways to promote your website

 HF5415.1265 .S93 1999

 005.2'76--dc21

99-6004

CIP